MW00438229

"Scores of Evangelic .... ory and been enlightened. They are amazed at the truth hidden from them and have taken the big step — they've entered the Catholic Church. They've stepped into a joyful new world and a wonderfully fresh experience. Now what? Are they prepared for their new adventure once inside the family? Shaun McAfee has provided a marvelous roadmap for what to expect and what to do next. From his own experience as a convert he shines a light along the path for new Catholics — and for old as well. His sage advice is must-read for all Catholics; it will make the Christian life in the Catholic Church come alive for us all."

— **Steve Ray**, Catholic evangelist
and writer at CatholicConvert.com

"Shaun McAfee has packed this little book full of tidbits for the inquisitive Catholic — protecting marriage, defending the Faith, avoiding pitfalls, and all manner of practical advice. He combines his wealth of experiences and travels to show how engaging Catholicism can be!"

— **Stacy Trasancos**, Catholic convert,
speaker, educator, and author

"Over the years, I have heard many converts lament the fact that there really is no 'how-to' manual to answer the inevitable 'what now' questions that arise the day after Easter Vigil and beyond. Finally, that book has arrived! Shaun McAfee has done that and more. *I'm Catholic. Now What?* answers those crucial 'how-to' and 'what now' questions along with presenting a wealth of apologetics that answers the also-crucial questions of 'why?' Why do we believe this? Why do we do that? It is precisely that trifecta of information that makes this book a must-read for all Catholics, not just new converts."

— **Tim Staples**, Director of Apologetics and
Evangelization at Catholic Answers

I'M CATHOLIC. NOW WHAT?

I'M CATHOLIC. NOW WHAT?

Shaun McAfee

Our Sunday Visitor
Huntington, Indiana

Nihil Obstat
Msgr. Michael Heintz, Ph.D.
Censor Librorum

Imprimatur
✠ Kevin C. Rhoades
Bishop of Fort Wayne-South Bend
October 20, 2019

The *Nihil Obstat* and *Imprimatur* are official declarations that a book is free from doctrinal or moral error. It is not implied that those who have granted the *Nihil Obstat* and *Imprimatur* agree with the contents, opinions, or statements expressed.

Except where noted, the Scripture citations used in this work are taken from the *Revised Standard Version of the Bible — Second Catholic Edition* (Ignatius Edition), copyright © 1965, 1966, 2006 National Council of the Churches of Christ in the United States of America. Used by permission. All rights reserved.

Every reasonable effort has been made to determine copyright holders of excerpted materials and to secure permissions as needed. If any copyrighted materials have been inadvertently used in this work without proper credit being given in one form or another, please notify Our Sunday Visitor in writing so that future printings of this work may be corrected accordingly.

Copyright © 2019 by Shaun McAfee

24 23 22 21 20 19   1 2 3 4 5 6 7 8 9

All rights reserved. With the exception of short excerpts for critical reviews, no part of this work may be reproduced or transmitted in any form or by any means whatsoever without permission from the publisher. For more information, visit: www.osv.com/permissions.

Our Sunday Visitor Publishing Division, Our Sunday Visitor, Inc., 200 Noll Plaza, Huntington, IN 46750, www.osv.com; 1-800-348-2440

ISBN: 978-1-68192-565-3 (Inventory No. T2025)
1. RELIGION—Christianity—Catholic. 2. RELIGION—Reference.
3. RELIGION—Christian Life—Personal Growth.

eISBN: 978-1-68192-566-0
LCCN: 2019949798

Cover design: Amanda Falk
Cover art: Shutterstock and Restored Traditions
Interior design: Amanda Falk

PRINTED IN THE UNITED STATES OF AMERICA

Dedicated to:
Beth and Mike Jareske, and Sean Stevens

*Thank you for setting me on
such an incredible journey.*

Contents

Read This First

Before diving in, I want to give you a huge welcome to the Catholic Church. Or maybe you're coming back to the Church — welcome! No matter your background, upbringing, or demographic, I am personally invested in making sure you get off the ground right, and that you always know that this is your family. And if you're a lifelong Catholic reader, thank you for your fidelity to the Faith.

While I was in RCIA, I was pretty sure I wanted to join the Catholic Church. But I wasn't totally sure I would be a "good Catholic," taking part in the sacraments, really preparing myself for Mass, or even following the liturgy terribly well. Like a small child, I wanted my basic needs met and my basic questions answered. If you had given me this book, I would likely have said, "That's great, but Jesus is all I need."

That sentiment was strongly rooted in my Evangelical upbringing, and probably enhanced by the popular culture that offers a so-called happy life full of pleasure and enjoyment. I would have asked, "Why do we even need to choose this denomination or that? We could do so much more together. I wish Catholics didn't spend their time talking about the 'extras.' Wouldn't it be better if we all just got along and respected each other's opinions and focused on the bigger reality that we are all following?"

You might be pondering these questions as well. They are valid. But what we want to avoid, whenever possible, is reductionism. We don't want to ask, "What's the least I can do?" Enjoying the fullness of the Catholic Faith means Catholics are free to enjoy the fullness of the *mission* of evangelism and the sacraments.

Here's what I was correct about: Jesus really is the one all Christians follow. However, Jesus gave the closest of his disciples, the apostles, his own authority (see Mt 16:18, 18:18). They were to convert the world and baptize people too. What does this mean for us? We converted, we have been baptized (or plan to be baptized); what more is there to do? Jesus did not just give the apostles authority and send them off to twiddle their thumbs. Jesus gave his disciples very specific teachings — so specific that their lives were in danger for defending them. He taught them that he was God (Jn 8:58–59); he taught them about the power of baptism (Jn 3:3); he taught them to consecrate bread and wine into his body and blood for us to consume (Mt 26:26; Jn 6:53); he gave them authority and instructed them to forgive sins (Jn 20:22–23); and so much more. Are these commands from the Son of God all "extra"? The answer is no, they're not "extra"; they're exclusive! When Jesus says, "Follow me" and appoints successors, he is telling us to follow him in and through those successors and the things he taught them.

This is an enriching feeling. When we learn about Jesus, the sacraments, and the facets of Christian virtue and morality, we are receiving a message Jesus planned for us close to two thousand years ago. That message has not changed in two millennia, but along the way, God has revealed to his saints and his faithful the many ways we can go about living out his teachings in order to perfect our souls. That's what the book you're holding is all about: helping you perfect your soul by living out the fullness of the Christian life. When you're reading this book, expel the temptation to do the minimum. Be an all-out Catholic! Do everything you can do — the easy and the hard, the delightful and the intimidating — and seek Jesus Christ through the highs and lows with the utmost sincerity and endurance.

***

When I was seven or eight years old, I was a very poor reader, because I had a lot of trouble focusing on what I was reading. My parents encouraged me to find a book that I actually wanted to read, something that would hold my attention. So I scanned the library for a good title and a good cover (because that's how you judge a good book, right?). I found a fantastic book! It was titled *How to Steal Your Sister's Diary*. This was going to be the best book I ever read, perhaps the most important, because I had an older sister who kept one of those fancy diaries with a little lock on it. And she hid it well enough that I never saw it unless she was journaling, or diary-ing, or whatever it's called.

I checked out the book, brought it home, and showed it to everyone. My sister laughed. She didn't look worried at all. Though she did promise to beat me up if she found out I read — let alone stole — her diary.

Just five or ten pages into the book, though, I was upset. This was not the book I thought I checked out. The title clearly said: "How to Steal Your Sister's Diary." But this book didn't explain anything about how to go about locating the diary, how to make sure said sister doesn't know, and how to break into and read said diary. I felt betrayed! As it turns out, it was a bright title for a novel about a brother who doesn't get along with this sister, but this and that happens, and he learns to love her. Sweet story, but the moral is that knowing what I was getting myself into would have helped; and that's what I want to make sure to do for you as you dive into this book.

You don't have to read front to back, but I do hope that, eventually, you read the whole book. You could read it front to back, or back to front, or dog-ear a thing or two that looks interesting. You can even flip through the book and stop to learn something that sticks out to you. Any formula will work, because every suggestion is aimed at helping you receive graces, grow in faith, and continue on the straight and secure road of communion with the Catholic Church, with heaven as the end goal.

I should mention, too, that even if you're not a Catholic yet, there are still many items for you in the book. Some examples are learning how to make an "examination of conscience" to better prepare you for confession, or how best to prepare for a wholesome pilgrimage, or how to defend against modern ideologies that conflict with our faith.

Finally, I suggest you keep this book close. The items here might take months or years to accomplish in aggregate — Catholicism is, after all, a lifetime adventure. The particular suggestions in this book, though, are what you need to get started. Pray as you go through every section to discern how to prioritize, and keep the book close for times when you're wondering, "What's next?" or "What was that again?"

Hopefully, this text will be practically helpful for you. Please enjoy, and share with a friend, a future convert, or someone who's already Catholic and is looking for more to do and know.

Getting Started

1
License to learn

While earning my undergraduate degree in aeronautics, I was required to obtain a private pilot's license. At first, I didn't see the point. I was an aircraft maintainer by trade, thanks to my time in the Air Force, and I was seeking a degree that concentrated on aviation management. If I wanted to fly anything, I wanted to fly a desk. Still, I proceeded with the program.

I distinctly remember my first flight. We had just lifted off when my flight instructor said, "Your controls."

"He just gave me a plane!" was all I could think. The thrill of flying has never escaped me since that moment. But to rewind: He didn't give me controls thirty minutes after meeting me. Before that, we spent hours together going over controls, the specs and operation of the aircraft, checklists and emergency procedures, and simulator time, in addition to the six to nine hours a week of ground school I had been required to complete.

Months later, I was ready to complete the grueling oral, written, and flight tests. By the end, I had just under fifty hours of flight time, over 120 hours in ground school, another twenty hours in a sim, countless other hours memorizing my checklists and "chair flying," and all the pre- and post-flight planning and briefing. I passed and earned my license, but the last thing my flight instructor said to me is something I'll never forget: "Shaun, you're a rated pilot now, but this is like someone just teaching you to walk. You're not ready to run on a team, you're not ready to sprint in competitions, and you're not ready to fly wherever, whatever, how high, and how fast you want. This license is a license to learn."

What did I do with that license? I used it! With that initial private pilot's license, I was able to get several other ratings, from landing on water to different landing-gear configurations. Soon I would meet many other pilots and get plugged into the aviation community. I also did something critical: I took time to enjoy flying.

The same logic of the "license to learn" has proven true of my life as a Catholic. Just as the requirement to get a pilot's license provided a knowledge of the entire aviation industry, becoming a Catholic was vital to my receiving a fuller understanding of Christ's Church, the sacraments, the natural law, and the journey to heaven. And as much as my new pilot's license was a "license to learn," baptism, confirmation, and my first Eucharist were the beginning of a journey. Just as I had a lot of learning ahead of me to be a knowledgeable, skilled, and experienced pilot, I had a lot of learning ahead of me to become a knowledgeable, virtuous, and wise Catholic.

I encourage you to look at your Catholic faith in this same way. Use your "license to learn"! Use it to grow in understanding theology, to build lifelong friendships, and most of all, to enjoy your faith. Catholicism *is* fun. It can be a little overwhelming, like landing at an unfamiliar airport and receiving unclear instructions, but our faith is enjoyable!

If you do find yourself overwhelmed, or if you haven't been in that proverbial cockpit for a while, don't panic; it takes some time to understand and to get situated in Catholicism. This is why we say that we "practice" our faith — to get better at it. The whole point of this book is to provide you with helpful guides and suggestions as you continue to practice and grow in your faith, utilizing your "license to learn" to its fullest extent.

2
Get a Bible and read it

The Catholic Church believes that the Bible is the Word of God and is useful for teaching. *Dei Verbum*, the Second Vatican Council's document on divine revelation, stresses:

> All the clergy must hold fast to the Sacred Scriptures through diligent sacred reading and careful study, especially the priests of Christ and others, such as deacons and catechists who are legitimately active in the ministry of the word. … The sacred synod also earnestly and especially urges all the Christian faithful, especially Religious, to learn by frequent reading of the divine Scriptures the "excellent knowledge of Jesus Christ" (Phil 3:8). "For ignorance of the Scriptures is ignorance of Christ." Therefore, they should gladly put themselves in touch with the sacred text itself, whether it be through the liturgy, rich in the divine word, or through devotional reading, or through instructions suitable for the purpose and other aids which, in

our time, with approval and active support of
the shepherds of the Church, are commendably
spread everywhere." (*Dei Verbum* 25)

Although the Church stresses the weight of Scripture and its regular reading, one of the most common Protestant critiques of Catholics is that we are biblically illiterate. Sadly, it is true that far too many Catholics really don't understand the Bible.

Regardless of who knows the Bible better, the basic fact is that Catholics and Evangelical Protestants use the Bible in different proportions and in different ways. A member of the congregation at a typical Evangelical Protestant service will access the Scriptures through a main passage (and other related individual verses) expounded on in a sermon. On any given Sunday, Catholics hear a lot more of the actual Scriptures, especially at Christmas and Easter Masses, where the readings are extended. Catholics and Evangelical Protestants use the Bible differently, too. Evangelical Protestants take the time to read it, because they believe that the Bible is the foundation and authority for God's specific revelation. They also believe that every believer — regardless of status or background — with the aid of the Holy Spirit, is capable of interpreting the Bible. In this way, Evangelicals use the Bible as a basis of authority and learning, whereas Catholics use the Bible, generally, as a book for worship and learning.

Here's the simple truth: If you want to be a Catholic of great faith and joy, one of your highest priorities should be to get a Bible (if you don't already have one) and read it regularly. Which Bible should you get? There are a lot to choose from, so here's a quick guide to some of the most popular Catholic versions:

- **Douay-Rheims Bible**. This was the standard English translation until the 1960s, and its powerful voice still grabs the reader's attention.

- **New American Bible (NABRE).** This is the most widely used Catholic Bible in the United States. Produced by the USCCB with the Catholic Bible Association, it is the translation that is used for Mass readings. It is a literal translation, and it generally reads well.

- **Revised Standard Version Catholic Edition (RSV-CE).** For its accuracy, ease, and readability, the RSV-CE has been the leading choice for scholars for most of the twentieth century and to the present. It is a very literal translation, which is preferred by many.

- **New Jerusalem Bible (NJB).** This is a "dynamic equivalence" translation, and its effect on its reader is meant to be roughly the same as the effect of the source text on its source reader. This makes the NJB a readable and accurate translation. The humble use of inclusive language gives this translation a special feel, and many readers appreciate the poetic sections.

There are still others, but we won't cover them here. Did you realize so many translations exist? Whatever Bible you choose, do not let it collect dust. Instead, use your Bible for study, reflection, and prayer.

Studying will help you become more religiously and biblically literate, which will give you a better appreciation for salvation history — God's continual intervention in history to save mankind. It will also give you a basis for knowing why you believe what you believe; and from this, you'll grow in the ability to defend your faith, which we'll talk more about in part 8, "Knowing and Defending your Faith."

Reflecting on Scripture is, perhaps, even more important than study. This means reflecting on what God wants to say to you through his word. A common form of reflection is called *lectio divina* (Latin for "divine reading"). In *lectio divina*, we start with a selection of Scripture (perhaps a few verses long) and read it following four traditional steps: (1) *lectio* (reading), (2) *meditatio* (reflecting on the words), (3) *oratio* (praying with the words and asking God what he wants to tell you in this reading), and (4) *contemplatio* (resting in God and listening for whatever he may have to tell you). *Lectio divina* produces much spiritual fruit and a deepened understanding of and love for the word of God.

As Catholics, we firmly believe that the Bible is God's word; if we really want to know God and what he wants, this is the place to find him.

3

Know your way around the *Catechism*

A catechism is a summary of the teachings of the Church. Catholics have always had catechisms. The very first catechism was a first-century manuscript called *The Didache* (or "the teaching"), which contained basic instruction on the Christian faith and rituals such as baptism and fasting, as well as teachings on the Christian life. Since then, catechisms have always been used by the faithful.

One of the most extraordinary works produced by the Church for the faithful is the 1992 *Catechism of the Catholic Church* (CCC). It is a reference containing the teachings of the Catholic Church. Its main purpose is to provide a universal reference for bishops and pastors, but it is also a helpful resource for all Catholics, from those who are just learning the precepts to theologians who wish to confirm and develop various articles of the Catholic Faith. Although it is not exhaustive in explaining every iota of theological thought expressed by the Church throughout the centuries, it provides information on nearly any topic one might want to research.

The *Catechism* is structured in an easy-to-read format, distilling the teachings of the Church into short paragraphs. The topics covered range from the sacraments and liturgy, to heaven and hell (and purgatory), angels and demons, and how the Church handles Scripture and Tradition. The *Catechism* is arranged in four general parts:

- The Profession of Faith (the Apostle's Creed)
- The Celebration of the Christian Mystery (the Sacred Liturgy, and especially the sacraments)
- Life in Christ (including the Ten Commandments)
- Christian Prayer (including the Lord's Prayer)

If you have not yet taken a look at the *Catechism*, be prepared to feel a little overwhelmed: It is a massive volume. This is because it provides a one-stop shop for almost any question on faith, morals, and the Christian life. So, how should you read it? I recommend first tracking down the much shorter *Compendium to the Catechism of the Catholic Church*. The *Compendium* is the summary of the *Catechism*, which can be a lot less daunting as you're starting out. You might also find it helpful to read the *Compendium* alongside the *Catechism*.

You might consider reading the *Catechism* cover to cover — over the long term. Break it down into sections and plan to read through it over the course of the next year or two. Really, this is the best way to ensure you don't skip any of the pertinent details. It also provides an enormous appreciation for the content and development of our faith, because the *Catechism* frequently pulls from other sources of the Magisterium, such as ecumenical councils, constitutions, works of saints and Church Fathers, papal encyclicals, and the Bible.

A straight reading might seem like an impossible undertaking — perhaps you've tried and failed to read the Bible cover to cover — so you might consider this alternative: Keep the *Catechism* close by and look up a topic you are interested in when the time comes. If something comes to mind, look it up. Maybe your friend has questions about the Catholic Church, and you don't have answers. Brush up by turning to the appropriate paragraph. Another good idea is to look up the daily readings in the Index of Citations.

How do you go about getting yourself a copy of the *Catechism*? You can purchase one online, or at your local Catholic bookstore. Perhaps you could ask your parish priests or deacons if they have an extra to spare. You can also access the *Catechism* for free online through the Vatican.va website, and through scborromeo.org. Both sites offer great navigation features. If you're willing to make the scholar's investment, Verbum software for phone and computers is the best way to cross-reference the *Catechism* with the many quoted documents of the Magisterium.

4

Know (and practice) the precepts of the Church

People often think of the Catholic Church as imposing countless rules and regulations. In reality, all Catholics must observe a few simple, "baseline" rules. These are called the precepts of the Church. By now, you've probably heard the term "practicing Catholic"; this refers to someone who faithfully observes the precepts of the Roman Catholic Church.

The *Catechism of the Catholic Church* enumerates the precepts in paragraphs 2042–2043. While this book covers them here in summary, you should read the full sections of the *Catechism* in your spare time. These are the precepts:

1. You shall attend Mass on all Sundays and on holy days of obligation.
2. You shall confess your sins at least once a year.
3. You shall receive the Sacrament of the Eucharist at least once during the liturgical season of Easter.
4. You shall observe the days of fasting and abstinence established by the Church.

5. You shall help to provide for the needs of the Church.

The Church names these precepts to keep us spiritually alive. Of course, the precepts are the minimum. Coming from a non-Catholic background, I can relate to anyone who upon first glance might think to themselves, *That's it? Too easy.* It's important to note that keeping these precepts is the baseline requirement for practicing the Faith, not the end goal. But new Catholics should know that the precepts are not alternatives for the Christian obligation of living a life of love and virtue (Jn 13:34) and the missionary work of evangelization given to all Christians (Mt 28:19–20).

5

Don't be afraid to genuflect

Some of the things that we do as Catholics can seem odd, elit-ist, or even silly, but I assure you, we do the things we do for a reason. You might not immediately understand the purpose of genuflecting before the tabernacle or kneeling in Mass, for ex-ample, and you might not even like it, but there are real reasons for these actions.

We'll go more into Catholic gestures and courtesies in more detail in part 6, but in broad terms, they're given to us to create and sustain unity. We say in the Creed, "I believe in one, holy, catholic, and apostolic church," and that oneness — unity — is vital. One key way we express it is through our outward behavior.

Consider the military. Military personnel wear the same uniform, eat the same meals, get the same haircut, and are re-quired to pass the same tests of knowledge and physical exer-tion. They have a strict and comprehensive understanding of who their leaders are, and also how to address them. This uni-formity is there for a reason: It instills discipline. The first thing soldiers learn to do as individuals and as a team is to march in formation — walking in a straight line, pivoting on the correct foot, and stopping when told. This is day-one stuff, but it's also ongoing in the formation of a soldier and a unit. It builds cohesion through discipline, which leads to better communication, which leads to better teamwork, and ultimately to victory. In the Catholic Church, what we want is victory over sin and the devil, and it's the unity of discipline, even in the smallest signs, that helps get us there.

This is why even the small gestures we make as Catholics are so important. Genuflection, for example, might seem like an option or "extra" formality, but it's an important action that reminds us of the Real Presence of Christ in the Eucharist. Be on your guard to practice these gestures and actions as often as you can. Sure, you might forget to bow once in a while, but stay on top of the norms as much as you can. When in doubt, peek at the missal and the Order of the Mass to be sure you're doing it right, and ask questions if you're unsure.

The Church asks us to genuflect, cross ourselves, kneel, trace crosses on our lips, etc., because these gestures are proper to the dignity of the liturgy and Real Presence in the Eucharist, and also for uniformity. If we fail to safeguard these courtesies, it becomes easier to make excuses for not protecting the essential parts of the way we demonstrate our faith together. And if we can't demonstrate our faith together, then we soon take on alterations to that faith. As Catholics, we are engaged in a very real spiritual battle for souls. Our main weapons are truth and the love of Christ, but consistency and unity are essential to winning the victory.

6

Heaven is the goal

The most important question one can ask seems so simple, yet it can be answered in so many different ways: "How do I get to heaven?" Some posit that we simply need to "accept Jesus as our personal Lord and Savior!" Others provide highly technical explanations on the nature of grace, cooperation, and sin. What's the Catholic response? While answers will vary, we do have a solid formula, and you should know it.

The "formula" boils down to this: To go to heaven, we must be baptized (1 Pt 3:21), repent of our sins (Mk 1:14–15), and have faith (Hb 11:6). As you live out your life as a Catholic, this formula will help you through moments of doubt or struggle, and you will find it to be an effective tool when defending the Church's teaching.

This formula really stems from Jesus' constant invitation to "Come, follow me!" Jesus' invitation is the answer to our question. But what does it mean to follow him all the way to heaven? The answers lie throughout Scripture, and they boil down to this: We must trust him with our whole life and give up everything we have to follow him (see for example Mk 10:17–27).

If we commit a mortal sin, which severs our relationship

with God, we must repent, have faith, and go to confession. Paul was unquestionably clear on the treatment of mortal sin, writing: "Do not be deceived; neither the immoral, nor idolaters, nor adulterers, nor homosexuals, nor thieves, nor the greedy, nor drunkards, nor revilers, nor robbers will inherit the kingdom of God" (1 Cor 6:9–10).

Though this basic formula is right and just, there is a deeper reality that all Christians must face if they wish to go to heaven: intention. Jesus makes this clear: "Not everyone who says to Me, 'Lord, Lord,' shall enter the kingdom of heaven, but he who does the will of My Father in heaven. Many will say to Me in that day, 'Lord, Lord, have we not prophesied in Your name, cast out demons in Your name, and done many wonders in Your name?' And then I will declare to them, 'I never knew you; depart from Me, you who practice lawlessness!'" (Mt 7:21–23).

When we speak of "intention," we mean the condition of your heart. God sees through vain repetition, mere religiosity, and an ingenuine friendship with him. Getting to heaven is not a matter of checking off boxes, but of doing God's will. This begins with baptism, repentance, and faith. If we do these things and follow Jesus in faith to the end, everything else will fall into place.

7

Knowledge isn't holiness

When I became a Catholic, I was very confused and dissatisfied with modern evangelicalism. The stage presence overtaking worship in the larger churches — cameras swinging over the crowd, smoke machines and light shows — showed a general lack of reverence that began to irk me. The same messages were repeated endlessly, and while some of the studies were engaging and eye-opening, those preaching weren't willing to tackle difficult topics. In short, it was a lot of fluff. Even worse, as I went from church to church, the preachers agreed only on the most basic things.

Because of this, a firm grasp of Church teaching, theological and moral, was of the utmost importance to me. I had to be comfortable in the new faith I was pursuing, and I had a lot of things to relearn. Along the way, too, I was confronted by friends, family, and acquaintances; I could either describe my new Catholic faith as a world of gray, or a bright and brilliant truth handed down and developed century by century since the age of the apostles. I wanted the latter, so I studied endlessly, learning as much as I could from the modern and older apologists and theologians. Plus, let's face it: Apologetics is exciting. There's nothing like knowing what you're talking about, and there are few things more satisfying than knowing what you believe is the unquestionable truth.

I studied for years, but when I began to read the lives of the saints, I quickly realized that I had a long way to go in knowledge and expertise. More importantly, I also realized that all the information I was accumulating wasn't contributing to my personal holiness. I could know everything, memorize all the reasons, and recite the Gospels if necessary, but until I let all of these change me, it was fruitless. It was like memorizing a recipe book but never learning how to choose ingredients, use the right kitchen tools, or serve a meal properly, and never being nourished.

Remember King Solomon of the Old Testament, said to have been the wisest man who ever lived? One would expect him to be wise enough to be holy, because by knowing so many things he would know the right choices to make, how to avoid sin, and how to love his neighbor. But he didn't. In all his wisdom, he failed to be holy. And because of this, the mighty kingdom his father, King David, built became infected by his obsession with personal gain.

It's great to continue to gain knowledge about Catholicism, but more importantly, your faith needs to grow. My suggestion for you is to balance the information that contributes to your knowledge with the information that contributes to your holiness. Even Satan knows what the Catholic Church teaches (which is why he is bent on sowing confusion to cause schisms within the Body of Christ). Merely knowing the Catholic Faith will not make you holy, and it will help you to be holy only if you allow it to change you.

Reading the writings and lives of the saints can help you extract those morsels of wisdom that will get you to heaven. They give you an example of what true wisdom looks like — the kind that leads to holiness. There's a story about Saint Thomas Aquinas, considered the most learned man in the history of the Church, who was praying when Jesus spoke to him from the crucifix, saying, "You've written well of me, Thomas. What do you want as your reward?" And Saint Thomas answered, *"Non nisi te, Domine. Non nisi te"* ("Nothing but you, Lord. Nothing but you").

Hopefully, you learn this lesson quickly, because time is a gift, and holiness takes time. Remember that it is more important to get to heaven than to know everything there is to know about heaven; knowing it all doesn't mean you're going there.

8

Remember that the Church is perfect, but her members aren't — yet

When we recite the Creed in unison each Sunday at Mass, we say, "I believe in one, *holy*, catholic, and apostolic Church." This can be difficult to accept. How can the Church be holy while she is simultaneously filled with and led by imperfect sinners? Do these two ideas contradict each other? No they don't, though some explanation is in order.

The identity of the Church as holy comes from the holiness of her founder: Christ. The *Catechism* explains: "'The Church ... is held, as a matter of faith, to be unfailingly holy. This is because Christ, the Son of God, who with the Father and the Spirit is hailed as "alone holy," loved the Church as his bride, giving himself up for her so as to sanctify her; he joined her to himself as his body and endowed her with the gift of the Holy Spirit for the glory of God.' The Church, then, is 'the holy People of God,' and her members are called 'saints'" (823).

The Church's identity is directly linked to her mission to

make everything holy: "United with Christ, the Church is sancti-fied by him; through him and with him she becomes sanctifying. 'All the activities of the Church are directed ... to the sanctifica-tion of men in Christ and the glorification of God.' It is in the Church that 'the fullness of the means of salvation' has been de-posited. It is in her that 'by the grace of God we acquire holiness'" (CCC 824).

Here's the bottom line: The Church is holy because Christ is holy. We share in the work of Christ, and therefore also in the identity of Christ: holy. Sometimes, because of our fallen condi-tion, we imperfectly participate in this work, and thus we also are imperfectly sanctified. But our imperfections do not cause a blemish on Christ's perfection, who is our unshakable identity.

The Church is somewhat of an oxymoron, however. She is meant to uphold and model the highest morals and virtues, but everywhere and in every historical moment we find forms of corruption, malaise, laziness, and abuse. There have been incred-ible highs in the Catholic Church, peaks of unfathomable mir-acles and holiness, but the lows in the Church can be miserable, vile, and downright embarrassing. We are expected to be model citizens, bearers of truth and goodness, but when we fall, we fall hard. And when we fail, we have epic fails.

It will happen to you, soon and often: You will encounter Catholics, perhaps even in positions of authority, who do not meet the Christian standard. Some will disappoint you. And some might fail you completely. When this happens, as fellow Christians and sinners, we are called to forgive them, pray, and look in the mirror.

You have prayed, perhaps hundreds of times, "Forgive us our trespasses, as we forgive those who trespass against us." These words of Jesus are even more to the point: "If you do not forgive men their trespasses, neither will your Father forgive your tres-passes" (Jn 6:15). When you encounter imperfect people in the

Church, strive to forgive them wholeheartedly, and don't forget to pray also for them to seek forgiveness.

Prayer is essential, and it is far more than mere wishful thinking or passive engagement. Who better to trust than the Father when someone in the family fails? Who better to correct a wrong than the Master? Prayer (see Part Four) is the most efficient means of eliminating sin and overcoming evil.

Finally, look in the mirror. It's ridiculously easy to point the finger at others, but it's harder to admit our own failings. As Christ puts it:

> Judge not, that you be not judged. For with the judgment you pronounce you will be judged, and the measure you give will be the measure you get. Why do you see the speck that is in your brother's eye, but do not notice the log that is in your own eye? Or how can you say to your brother, "Let me take the speck out of your eye," when there is the log in your own eye? You hypocrite, first take the log out of your own eye, and then you will see clearly to take the speck out of your brother's eye. (Mt 7:1–5)

When we find the people in the Church to be less than perfect — perhaps complete failures — we can look to the cross, because the forgiveness, prayer, and humility that Jesus demonstrates for us are sure paths to healing.

What does this mean for you and your own growth toward holiness? Well, first, it should motivate you. Jesus is the one who makes you holy; you don't have to get there all by yourself. Second, it should equip you with enormous confidence: Jesus, who is God, has invited you to continue in his work of sanctification, bringing sinners to salvation. Because we are part of this holy

Church, given the mission to bring Christ's salvific work to others, we have every reason for confidence in the success of our work.

Allow Holy Mother Church to aid you in your journey to sanctification and your mission of sharing the message of salvation.

The Sacraments

9

Live the sacraments

You can probably name all the seven sacraments, and you might have recently received a few of them. That's good, but knowing about them is not enough — at the end of our lives, there won't be a pop quiz that decides whether or not we get to heaven.

Instead, we have been given a law to abide by — a map for getting to heaven. We know this as the Law of Love, the Law of the Gospel, or the New Covenant. This law is love, charity, and selfless devotion to others. Love is the greatest law — the one that sums up all others. But being loving is not as easy as it seems. We need help with it, and we also need help being good and recovering from our sins. The sacraments enable us to access the graces God wants to give us, leading to a Godly love for others and a faithful working out of our salvation. As the *Catechism* summarizes: "The New Law is the *grace of the Holy Spirit* given to the faithful through faith in Christ. It works through charity; it uses the Sermon on the Mount to teach us what must be done and makes use of the sacraments to give us the grace to do it" (1966).

Going through life without the sacraments is like trying to

eat a five-course dinner blindfolded and with your hands tied behind your back — it's not impossible, but it's going to be messy. That's an imperfect analogy, but you get the idea. The sacraments enable us to actively participate in the life of Christ. And, as the *Catechism* notes, these sacraments are "necessary for salvation" — a statement that should immediately grab our attention (1129). The *Catechism* says:

> Celebrated worthily in faith, the sacraments confer the grace that they signify. They are *efficacious* because in them Christ himself is at work: it is he who baptizes, he who acts in his sacraments in order to communicate the grace that each sacrament signifies. The Father always hears the prayer of his Son's Church which, in the epiclesis of each sacrament, expresses her faith in the power of the Spirit. As fire transforms into itself everything it touches, so the Holy Spirit transforms into the divine life whatever is subjected to his power. (1127)

When we're eating that five-course dinner, we want it to make us happy; we want it to be nourishing and healthy; we want to pay a fair price; and we want good company. Living a sacramental life is similar. It is our foretaste here on earth of the wedding banquet in heaven.

The rest of this section provides practical suggestions aimed at helping you make the most of the sacraments, especially the two you will encounter the most regularly in your life: confession and the Holy Eucharist. These two sacraments are the one-two that you should plan to receive many times throughout your life. (The minimum requirement is once a year for each.) Let's start with confession.

10

Know how to make a good confession

There is no limitation to the frequency that you may receive absolution for sins, but the quality is profoundly important for us to receive all the possible graces of the sacrament. And when we're prepared beforehand, attentive in the confessional, and full of gratitude after we finish, these become lasting developments in our spiritual lives, and a solid foundation for further growth in holiness and communion with God. Here are a few practical means of being prepared, attentive, and grateful whenever we receive the Sacrament of Reconciliation.

MAKE A THOROUGH EXAMINATION OF CONSCIENCE

Confession takes place in the presence of a priest, but the sacrament begins with your personal examination of conscience. Here, you consider all the sins you have committed and all the things you've failed to do (known as sins of omission). It is usually easy to remember the big sins, but it's harder to remember the smaller sins. As you continue to grow in your faith, it is likely

44

you will discover sins you didn't know you committed or things you didn't know you were supposed to do (or not do). These are also good to bring to the sacrament to keep you aware for the future. When you're able to identify these, the sacrament is more effective in its secondary purpose: to enable you to eliminate sin from your life.

We should also consider our level of contrition, meaning how sorry we are for the sins we have committed. If we go to confession without contrition, we cannot receive God's forgiveness because we are not disposed to accept it. Sometimes we experience imperfect contrition, where we confess from a lesser motive such as fear of punishment or the fear of hell. This is a valid form of contrition, but our aim should be perfect contrition, in which we are sorry for disobeying God because we love him, and we completely resolve to avoid sin in the future. Perfect contrition comes from a perfect love of God.

Each time you approach the sacrament, you should also do a thorough examination of the time since your last confession (the more often you go, the easier it gets). The United States Conference of Catholic Bishops (USCCB) and Eternal Word Television Network (EWTN) both have many resources for different examinations of conscience tailored for young people, singles, children, spouses, and other states of life. Look for these online.

ELIMINATE DISTRACTIONS

When in the confession line, you really should clear yourself of all possible distractions. If you can, leave your cell phone in your car. You don't want to be checking Facebook, the score of the game, or the restaurant menu you'll have the chance to read later. You want to be distraction-free so that you can consider your relationship with God more thoroughly, consider the ways the Holy Spirit wants to work in and through you, and prepare to make a sincere and fully contrite confession.

SLOW DOWN AND TAKE YOUR TIME

Don't rush the process. Appreciate being in line, even if it lasts a while. Don't like the size of the line? Use it as a means of penance. When it's your turn, reverently make the Sign of the Cross, reigniting your confidence in the work of the cross, recommitting to your baptismal promises, and fully trusting that when you exit the confessional, you will be entirely forgiven. Take your time to speak your sins by type and number to the priest, and don't forget to mention any sins of omission (like failing to pray, forgive, be merciful, etc.). Take your time and allow yourself to be fully open to the graces of this beautiful sacrament.

DON'T BE DEFENSIVE

Sometimes you might get a priest who takes the confessional as his opportunity to give teaching. Others desire to be encouraging, and still others will ask you questions. Every priest is different, but they are all trying to help you complete your confession, receive absolution, and sin no more. This might require a bit of understanding on your part, and holy patience, too. Whatever you do, remain humble and listen to what the priest is attempting to tell you.

DON'T LOOK FOR PRAISE

There are many subtle ways in which most of us seek praise or reassurance in the confessional. You might name your sins, but preface or conclude them with the things you did right. You might use complex theological words, or interrupt the priest to explain or excuse yourself or to supplement his advice. Don't caveat your sins and make them sound less severe. No matter how bad the sin, you are getting ready to receive Jesus Christ's complete and generous mercy. The best offering you can make of yourself is the offering of the centurion: "Lord, I am not worthy" (Mt 8:8). Stay humble. Period.

BE SPECIFIC

While slowing down your words, you also want to take the time you need to be specific about your sins. It is important to confess the specific sins you have committed in all their ugliness. What caused you to sin? Is there a time of day you regularly commit this sin? Is there a common thread to your giving in to temptation? It may be more painful, for example, to confess looking at pornography than to confess looking at women with lust, but it will benefit your soul and allow the priest to help you more. This honesty will grant you humility, courage, self-integrity, discipline, and more. Sin, like a disease, cannot be cured until it has been diagnosed accurately.

LEAVE OTHERS OUT OF IT

Here is a general and simple rule: Don't bring others into your confession. Don't speak of the sins of others to make yours look less damaging, or to offer evidence of how one of your sins might not be entirely your fault. This sacrament is about your soul and Jesus' love for you. Leave others out of your confession.

ABSOLUTION IS COMPLETE AND FINAL

You must have zero doubts about the finality of your absolution. Those sins are buried. Dead. They're never coming back. Ever. So don't think about them for a single moment longer! The work of the cross is unconditional — when we doubt that we are really forgiven, we are really doubting the authority of Christ; so don't do it. Have confidence in the graces given to you and be confident in the strength of the sacrament over the powers of darkness.

COMPLETE YOUR PENANCE

When it comes to making amends for our sins, the penance given in confession plays an important role. The *Catechism* states:

"Absolution takes away sin, but it does not remedy all the disorders sin has caused. Raised up from sin, the sinner must still recover his full spiritual health by doing something more to make amends for the sin: he must 'make satisfaction for' or 'expiate' his sins. This satisfaction is also called 'penance'" (1459).

Yes, it's easy to forget or otherwise neglect to complete your penance. One time I walked out of the confessional to my wife, who handed me our newborn so she could go into the confessional herself. I got distracted, and I forgot my penance. Another time, a priest gave me a specific activity to perform during the week, and I completely forgot about it for several days. Don't allow forgetfulness to discourage you, but do your best to guard against it. Usually your penance will be something small, so it's easy to lose sight of how important it is. Whatever the priest assigns, take it seriously and don't forget to do it.

11

Go to confession regularly

The Sacrament of Reconciliation is not a penalty — it is a gift, a privilege, as are all of the sacraments. But going to confession can be somewhat hectic and stressful. Figuring out when the "light is on" in your parish or neighborhood, standing in line, and telling your most personal secrets to a stranger (or maybe a family friend) is not comfortable. But regular confession is a source of amazing, unfathomable graces.

The Catholic Church requires that each one of us visit the Sacrament of Reconciliation at least once a year. As the *Catechism* says, "after having attained the age of discretion, each of the faithful is bound by an obligation faithfully to confess serious sins at least once a year" (1457). That's not very difficult, but it is the minimum, and it assumes that you're in a state of grace for nearly the whole year. In any case, a once-a-year visit to the confessional is not nearly enough to progress in virtue and devotion.

Confession is an opportunity not merely to correct sinful behavior, but also to correct neglect or apathy in our relationship with God, and to provide us with wisdom and tactics to win the spiritual battles in our lives. After all, we aren't just supposed to confess our mortal sins and what else we have done, but we also should acknowledge and admit what we lack and what we have failed to do.

We increase in virtue at an astonishing rate when we visit the sacrament regularly — many spiritual directors suggest once a month or every two weeks, especially if you're having trouble with habitual sins or you have a significant issue to discern. Honestly confessing sins, obtaining the sacramental graces that are so powerful for our souls, and receiving absolution is the best way to overcome sin, period.

Absolution and penance further aid our souls by giving us a chance to atone. Not to mention, some of the best advice you can receive is given in the confessional. Priests have heard it all, and they are profoundly equipped to render life-changing counsel to set us in the right direction.

There are plenty of reasons to visit the Sacrament of Reconciliation, and the more often we go, the better off we are. Make this a priority, no matter what sacrifices it requires.

UNCONFESSED AND FORGOTTEN SINS

When we're talking about the Sacrament of Confession, common questions arise about unconfessed and forgotten sins.

We know the rule: Confess all sins we can remember, particularly the mortal sins. It is the "remembering" that is especially important, which is why this book — and probably all spiritual directors worth their salt — recommends a frequent examination of conscience. This shines a light on things we have done but might otherwise forget.

Forgetfulness is one thing, but we need to avoid simply not confessing certain sins. Willfully failing to confess a mortal sin — withholding it or concealing it in the confessional — is itself a mortal sin, and it means we can't receive the priest's absolution. This new mortal sin adds to the disorder and lack of grace in our life. Picture it like bacteria, which starts as a microscopic infection and multiplies quickly. At first, it's undetectable to its host, but almost overnight we realize something is off. The smart person confronts the bacteria with an antidote and temporarily (or permanently) starves the bacteria of any chances of fighting or coming back. But the person who ignores the bacteria is in for a rude awakening. They're sick beyond all expectation, wondering how it happened so fast; they're immobilized and can't keep anything down. Soon its effects are noticeable to everyone, and like any disease, people don't want to be near the infected.

Unconfessed mortal sins are kind of like that bacteria. If you're ever wondering why your spiritual life is suddenly going haywire — and maybe your social, professional, and personal life, too — and you realize you've been withholding a mortal sin, go to a priest and confess it. Confession is the only antidote for mortal sin.

Then there are forgotten sins. These are a nuisance, but don't let them disturb your peace. Virtually everyone forgets sins, and in these cases, a valid absolution heals all sins, even unconfessed ones. Still, if you've been to confession and later remember something you forgot to bring up, you should mention it in a later confession. While the sin is forgiven and healed, the effects remain, and you must confess it to heal completely.

You might also consider, with the guidance of a trusted spiritual director, making a general confession. This practice allows you to look back over your whole life and confess everything, even sins you have already brought to confession. This practice can be especially beneficial at big moments of transition in your life (for instance, the Church recommends it for people preparing for religious vows). It's important to note, however, that the Church does not recommend making general confessions repeatedly, and you should not make one if you struggle with scrupulosity.

What is scrupulosity? It is anxiety about one's sins, which can lead a person to doubt the mercy and forgiveness of God. The scrupulous person is anxious that he has committed a sin when in fact he has not, or is convinced that his venial sins are mortal when they are not. This anxiety can lead to doubt of God's grace (in itself, a grave sin). Thoroughness is good, but being overscrupulous is a hazard to be avoided. If you find yourself struggling with scrupulosity, speak with a priest or trusted spiritual director. As an added protection against scrupulosity, try to go to confession to the same priest regularly. The familiarity will provide the opportunity to gain clarity about sins for which you have already received absolution.

12

Get to Mass on time
and stay till the end

The rules for Mass are simple: "Sunday, on which by apostolic tradition the paschal mystery is celebrated, must be observed in the universal Church as the primordial holy day of obligation" (Canon 1246.1). As the *Catechism* clarifies: "Those who deliberately fail in this obligation commit a grave sin" (2181). Here, I'll add the words of the late Father Ray Ryland:

> The utter folly of what we do by willfully ignoring our Mass obligation is somewhat analogous to a deep-sea diver's putting a crimp in his airline so that no air can come through to keep him alive. By a decision to miss Sunday Mass or a holy day of obligation we suspend the operation of sanctifying grace in our lives. For the sake of our eternal salvation, we must go to confession in true contrition as soon as possible and take the crimp out of our airline, so to speak, allowing sanctifying grace again to flood our souls.[1]

But our Sunday Mass attendance should not simply be a matter of showing up. We should also prioritize being on time. Does this mean Mass doesn't count if you're late? Not necessarily. Yet the truth is, every single part of the Mass is vital. There are no extras in the Mass; everything is there for a good reason. If you find you are consistently running into Sunday Mass late, rather than trying to determine how late is "too" late, I encourage you to try to figure out why you are late in the first place.

I've been late for reasons ranging from rounding up kids, to lost car keys, to poor traffic. If we are delayed because of circumstances that we cannot control, then we still fulfill our obligation, even if we show up to Mass late. You might find yourself in a situation where you had the service time wrong, and it caused you to walk in on a Mass that was already in progress. Of course, there will always be the rare occasion when something goes wrong and you're late. Arriving late to Mass becomes a problem when it is the result of negligence or because we would rather not be there at all. In these cases, we have not fulfilled our Mass obligation in any real spirit of the law.

What can you do if you're frequently late? Start by making adjustments to your pre-Mass routine. This could be the time you eat breakfast, the time you start getting ready, or the route you take to the church. Make the needed adjustments to establish a regular routine of being on time to Mass. Don't be afraid to be honest with yourself about the reasons why you're running late. Just like you would never want to arrive late to your friend's wedding, don't be late for the wedding banquet where we drink the wine of the New Covenant.

Perhaps a more significant concern than being late to Mass is leaving Mass right after Communion. If you're tempted to leave early, try to remember that the moments after receiving Communion are opportune for giving thanks, reflecting on the mysteries of the Eucharist, contemplating the paschal sacrifice, and resting in the presence of God. Besides, who wouldn't want to have a nice moment of quiet and rest?

Mass is one of the most important things you will ever participate in. Years ago, before I was Catholic, I was driving home on a Sunday morning in April in Fairbanks, Alaska. That morning, I was begging God to use me: "God, I am not doing anything meaningful with my life. When do I evangelize? Never! God, please give me an opportunity to help someone right now." Then there he was: a native Alaskan walking on the side of the Richardson Highway. If you've been to Alaska in April, you know it's still pretty cold outside. In a split second, I experienced a rush of thoughts: "Oh wow! There's a man out there!" "Should I give him a ride?" "I bet I won't be able to help him much, and he'll refuse my help anyway." Then it hit me: "Wait, didn't I just beg God to give me someone to help?"

I threw the car in reverse and backed in beside him. He immediately accepted my invitation. He was getting ready to travel on foot to a town maybe two hundred miles eastward. If that wasn't astonishing enough, he was dead set on getting to Mass before he left. He had walked fifteen miles that morning from the mine where he worked. He walked this whole way, in negative temperatures, just to get to Mass before he left town. I wasn't Catholic back then, but I drove him to the nearest parish, and then as far as I could reasonably take him.

Mass is important. Get there on time, don't leave early, and take the opportunity to soak up all the grace Christ wants to give you in his wedding banquet.

13

Where should you
sit for Mass?

All Catholics have to make the same decision when they get
to Mass: "Where should I sit?" You might sit with a friend or
with a family member or by yourself. That's all great. But whether
you're a new Catholic or have been Catholic and have attended
the same parish for years, you should always consider the place
where you sit and how it affects others.

First things first: If you arrive early, consider not sitting in
the end of the pew closest to the aisle. Yes, sitting on the aisle will
usually get you more space (sometimes even the whole pew clear
to the other aisle). It also ensures a quick exit, if you need one.
But both space and mobility are a trade-off on the fellowship
you're giving up and the presentation of an inviting parish. Moving in to the center of the pew to leave room for others is part
charm and part engagement, and it's a subtle method of evangelizing your parish.

Imagine someone who's visiting your parish for the first
time. They arrive right on time to a church that looks like it has
no seats left, when there's actually plenty of room if folks just

moved a space or two to the center of their pew. Those who are visiting or even thinking of joining the parish are going to feel much more at home if finding a place to sit isn't stressful. No one should be made to feel as if they're inconveniencing an entire pew just to find a place to sit for forty-five minutes. If you do sit near the aisle in your pew, try to be attentive to those who are looking for seats. Even if you prefer not to move into the center, as a sign of goodwill, offer the empty seats next to you in the pew.

Oh, and if you are new, strongly consider making your place up front. There, you'll literally see more of the Mass, hear more of the Mass, and be more focused on the Mass. I doubly stress this for families.

14

Receive holy Communion worthily

Receiving holy Communion is absolutely one of the most important things you will ever do: consuming the Body and Blood of your God. Our Lord's own words point to the truth that the Eucharist is vital to the Christian life:

> So Jesus said to them, "Truly, truly, I say to you, unless you eat the flesh of the Son of man and drink his blood, you have no life in you; he who eats my flesh and drinks my blood has eternal life, and I will raise him up at the last day. For my flesh is food indeed, and my blood is drink indeed. He who eats my flesh and drinks my blood abides in me, and I in him. As the living Father sent me, and I live because of the Father, so he who eats me will live because of me. This is the bread which came down from heaven, not such as the fathers ate and died; he who eats this bread will live forever." (Jn 6:53–58)

Receiving the Eucharist is essential for us as Catholics — the more often, the better. But we must receive it in the proper state (i.e., the state of grace). As Saint Paul says, "Whoever, therefore, eats the bread or drinks the cup of the Lord in an unworthy manner will be guilty of profaning the body and blood of the Lord" (1 Cor 11:27).

To receive Communion worthily, you must believe in transubstantiation, observe the Eucharistic fast, not be under an ecclesiastical censure such as excommunication, and, finally, be in a state of grace. Transubstantiation is a long word explaining the reality that the bread and wine transform, without changing their physical appearance, into the Body, Blood, Soul, and Divinity of Christ.

The Eucharistic or pre-Communion fast is a way of challenging each of us to observe the reality of Jesus' Real Presence in the Eucharist. The current Code of Canon Law (approved by Pope John Paul II in 1983) requires Catholics with no mitigating circumstances (like age, sickness, or pregnancy) "to receive the Most Holy Eucharist [and] abstain from any food or drink, with the exception of water and medicine, for at least the period of one hour before holy Communion."[2] After Communion, although there is no restriction on how soon you may break the fast, many people, as an act of reverence, choose not to eat or drink for fifteen minutes after receiving (which is about as long as the Host remains intact in your stomach).

Let's drill down on the last requirement for a worthy Communion: being in a state of grace. "State of grace" means that, at the minimum, you have not committed any mortal sins since your last confession.

It is often said that the Eucharist is the one sacrament that unites believers in the fullness of the Catholic Faith. Other sacraments may be administered as a matter of law, but the Eucharist uniquely binds believers as an act of faith. Because of what it is, it must be received properly.

It is tempting to receive holy Communion when I have not been to confession since committing a mortal sin. It is also easy to minimize sins, to push them way back in your memory, and receive Communion anyway. But to receive unworthily has infinitely more dangerous consequences than embarrassment, impatience, or willful ignorance. Faith and respect for the presence of the Lord require that we make the right choice to stay in the pew, or approach with our arms crossed over our chest for a simple blessing. Make every effort to be sure you are in a state of grace when receiving holy Communion.

15

Reserve Sundays for their true purpose

The Eucharist is the "source and summit of our faith." Our consumption of the bread and wine is the real consumption of the Body, Blood, Soul, and Divinity of Christ. However, the third commandment, "keep holy the Sabbath day," includes more than just going to Mass. It also includes marking the day with real rest.

I have always been the sole earner in my family, fulfilling a promise to my wife to enable her to stay at home and raise our children. We've made a lot of sacrifices to do that, and for a long time the principle I learned in college remained my personal philosophy: "Time is money, and money is time." Nobody could touch my time, so when a close friend, whom I deeply respected as a mentor in the Faith, suggested I rest on the Sabbath day, his suggestion fell on defensive ears.

I was writing, sponsoring in RCIA, earning a master's degree in theology, trying to make a difference in the world — and I couldn't clean my garage on a Sunday? Didn't my work earlier in the week somehow earn me some time to keep my house clean?

Doesn't the work I do for my home fall into some sort of "good works" category?

I had every excuse in the book, and I just wouldn't hear my friend. Then he reshaped his approach.

"Shaun, don't you want the day off? If you could work all day, or rest, reflect, and just have downtime with your family, wouldn't you do it?"

"Well … yeah. I would."

"Then why don't you?"

I gave him the only real and honest answer in me. "Because I have work to do, and I'm afraid that if I fall behind in any of it, it will just pile up."

The fact is, I was much more concerned with getting things done than attempting to remain obedient to a commandment that seemed to have no place in my modern life. I told him I would think about it, and I did. Was I really breaking one of the Ten Commandments? Playing it safe, I decided to give his advice a shot just for that day and check out every other Catholic resource I could find on the subject. In addition to obeying the Ten Commandments, we are also obliged to follow the precepts of the Church, the first of which builds off the third commandment. I found this in the *Catechism*:

> The first precept ("You shall attend Mass on Sundays and holy days of obligation and rest from servile labor") requires the faithful to sanctify the day commemorating the Resurrection of the Lord as well as the principal liturgical feasts honoring the mysteries of the Lord, the Blessed Virgin Mary, and the saints; in the first place, by participating in the Eucharistic celebration, in which the Christian community is gathered, and by *resting from those works and*

*activities which could impede such a sanctifica-
tion of these days.* (2042, emphasis added)

It's clear that there must be some rest involved in our Sundays, but what activities should we specifically avoid? Looking around some more, I found resources that confirmed and agreed with my friend's explanation. I developed a short checklist of questions to evaluate my desired "work":

1. Is [insert work here] completely necessary?
2. Does [insert work here] contribute to the sanctification of Sunday?
3. Is [insert work here] something I would/could ordinarily do on another day of the week?

As much as I didn't want to think about it, what was seriously at stake was the looming question: Was I really breaking one of the Ten Commandments?

Indeed I was — and my gosh, look where in the list this commandment is placed. It's the third commandment, the last element of the trilogy of commandments that explain the relationship God wants to have with each of us individually.

However, we shouldn't be legalistic over this matter. If you ever have trouble deciding if a particular activity is against your observation of Sunday, just ask yourself those three questions. And trust God to fulfill his promises and help you keep his day holy.

16

Try the Latin Mass

You might find it called the Latin Mass, the Traditional Latin Mass, or the Tridentine Mass (from the Council of Trent, where it was streamlined) — but it's most accurately called the Extraordinary Form of the Roman Rite. Your normal Mass, the one you will find most often, is appropriately known as the Ordinary Form. Fun fact: There are actually over twenty rites of the Mass! But we'll focus on the Extraordinary Form here, which, prior to the liturgical changes following the Second Vatican Council, was the ordinary celebration of the Mass.

I highly recommend that you pop over to an Extraordinary Form Mass at some point in your life. It's part of the precious heritage of our faith that has remained largely unchanged for centuries. Rooted in the form normalized by Saint Gregory the Great in the seventh century, it experienced variations in the medieval and Renaissance periods and was later solidified under a universal form by Pius V in 1570.

I love this form of the Mass because it is deeply reverent, its structure and tempo contain a delicious sense of connectedness with the liturgy and saints, and it's undeniably historical. When you go, you should know a few things. Only the sermon will be in English; there is no sign of peace among the congregation; the priest will face *ad orientem*; Communion is received only on the tongue while kneeling (unless you are physically unable), and you do not say "amen" prior to receiving. It's a good idea not to get bogged down in flipping pages and reading the English translations at first. Just sit back — well, follow what the people around you are doing — relax, and focus on the Lord.

17

Attend daily Mass

In this book we've already covered the precepts of the Church (see section 4), among which is the requirement to attend Mass each Sunday and on designated holy days of obligation. Eventually, you may feel inclined to attend Mass more often, a practice which is always encouraged. This is why most parishes, nearly everywhere you may live or travel, will offer daily Mass at least a few days a week.

Speaking from experience, I didn't know for some time that Mass is usually available every day of the week. At first, getting to Mass during the week seemed very difficult, but over time, I came to desire it; at points in my life, it has even become a habit. Even if I can't attend Mass every single day of the week, when I do make it, I find it is great for practical relief to take a time out in the middle of my workday. However, I sincerely want you to know that daily Mass is not a requirement and that you should never feel pressured to attend. It's far too easy to become scrupulous about it or to feel you are not being "Catholic" enough if you don't make daily Mass a priority. On the other hand, I sincerely want you to consider attending daily Mass when you feel the time is right.

The surface benefits of daily Mass are clear: You receive the graces of the Blessed Sacrament every time you go. Daily Mass is also the supreme approach to following the liturgical calendar. From the progression of the Scripture readings in discussing salvation, to the saints celebrated each day, daily Mass is really the key to getting plugged in to the liturgy. It is also a fine opportunity to receive the Sacrament of Reconciliation regularly, because many parishes will offer confession times before or after Mass on particular days of the week (some even offer confession before every Mass).

Remember, though, that every Catholic has different circumstances. For some, a move to the countryside diminishes the opportunity to attend daily Mass. Families with young children often find it difficult to attend Mass during the week. Sometimes, local parishes change schedule or lose priests or, for one reason or another, cannot offer a regular daily Mass schedule. If circumstances won't allow you to attend daily Mass, don't worry. Attending daily Mass is not a requirement, but a strong devotional practice to add to your prayer life when you are able. If you have a Catholic church nearby, but daily Mass is unavailable, talk to the pastor there to see if that can change. If you think it is warranted, you may even consider writing to the bishop to explain your local community's needs.

Another interesting thing happened after my conversion that's related to daily Mass, and I want you to experience it as well. Do this: Visit masstimes.org and run a search on your location to see how many parishes are nearby and when they offer the sacraments. Depending on where you live, you may be shocked to learn how available daily Mass actually is. Hopefully, you will also feel encouraged to make daily Mass — at least now and then — a part of your spiritual life.

18

Go to Eucharistic adoration

When I was in RCIA, one of the parish deacons took us on a tour of the church. Along the way, he explained the purpose of each area within the parish. He told us what the narthex is and what it's for, and then he did the same with the confessional, the sacristy, and even the parish library.

A special place he took us was directly behind the altar. This was the only place where he did not narrate while we were actually in the location. Instead, he first kept the door closed and explained, "When you walk through this door, here is what you will find. … Here's what people in here are doing. … This is when you can come back." Then we quietly and respectfully entered the Blessed Sacrament chapel. There were four parishioners quietly praying. Some didn't appear to be praying, but merely thinking or staring or just sitting.

They were each spending time in that little chapel to adore Christ's Real Presence in the Eucharist. It's called "Eucharistic adoration," and you've probably heard of it. Maybe you've been Catholic for some time and you want to participate. All you have to do is ask your priest when he presents the Eucharist for adoration (if it's not already printed in the bulletin or noted online). If your parish doesn't have adoration, look around — a church nearby will probably have adoration available. Many times, too, a parish will have a smaller chapel away from the main church and nave, where they have Eucharistic adoration often or even perpetually. In perpetual adoration chapels, the Host is always exposed (shown openly) except during the Easter Triduum. Perpetual adoration is a special means of giving constant adoration to the Creator. Simultaneously, it's a constant invitation from our Lord to stop by and visit him, whenever you can and for as long as you can. God gives special graces to those who spend time in front of the Eucharist.

I highly encourage you, the next time you're at your parish, to ask who is in control of the schedule for adoration. If you have access to a perpetual adoration chapel, consider taking over a regular time slot (usually one hour a week). Make sure before you make that commitment, though, that your schedule and state of life allow you to be ready and willing to follow through. As my RCIA sponsor told me, "Don't put too much pressure on yourself. Just stop in when you can."

What you should aim for is what's known as a "holy hour." It's exactly what it sounds like: a whole hour of adoration before the Blessed Sacrament. What do you do in adoration? First, let's discuss what not to do. Here are the ground rules:

- Try not to disturb (or distract) others. Avoid loud music and conversation, silence your cell phone, and try to close the door quietly.
- Remain aware of the sanctity of the chapel and the Real Presence there, modifying your dress and your behavior accordingly.
- Traditionally, when the Blessed Sacrament is exposed, one genuflects on both knees rather than the standard right-knee genuflection.
- Avoid technology that might distract others or

seem like a scandal. Many people use different apps that contain prayers, readings, and reflections — these are just fine. But if you plan to use some other technology that might distract others from prayer, you might want to take a brief moment to ask the other folks if they would not be disturbed by your device.

Now, what can you do during your adoration time? There's some general etiquette, but it's really up to you. You're above all encouraged to pray and reflect on the Real Presence and speak to Jesus as a friend. Many people bring something to read. It's an excellent choice to read Scripture (see section 2 on *lectio divina*), the lives and writings of the saints, reflections, or other spiritual readings. Many people pray the Rosary or the Divine Mercy chaplet during their holy hour. It is not unusual to find worshipers with headphones on low volume, listening to hymns, chant, or worship music (but keep in mind the ground rules above). Try your best to remain silent in the presence of Christ, focusing on good and holy things.

Even if you can't spend an hour, aim for something like thirty minutes a week, which is enough for a Rosary and some silent time. Even stopping in and praying for five minutes is better than five hours of binging on Netflix. So take the long way home next time, and stop in to say hello to your Redeemer. And if you're interested in perpetual adoration, ask around at your parish for the nearest coordinator, and they'll tell you everything you need to know.

19

Celebrate the day of your baptism

Birthdays are great, but Christianity considers two other days more important than your birthday: the days of your baptism and death. The two are essential for the same reason: They mark the start of a new life. One is a new life in this world, and the other is a new life in the next. This is why the Church almost always celebrates saints' feast days on the historical date of their death. It is also why there is a long-standing tradition to remember the solemnity of your baptism. If you're a parent or godparent, pay particularly close attention: Commemorate and honor the anniversary of the baptisms of your children and godchildren.

How can you do this? It's simple: Treat it like a feast day for the living. Send a small but holy gift to the baptized person. Pray for them. Pray with them. Send a card if you're not in the immediate locale, or call — or do both! Ask for a Mass to be offered for them.

Remembering someone's baptism day, especially a child's or godchild's, is an incredible act of spiritual encouragement. It's easy for young people to get lost in the distractions of adolescence, and even easier for adults to forget this significant anniversary. This makes it so much more special when someone remembers. It sets aside time to consider and discuss spiritual milestones, and it creates a perfect opportunity to rejoice in the mercies and graces of the sacraments. The event is literally life-changing, so make a substantial effort to set this date aside as something holy.

20

Pursue the graces of your marriage

As Catholics, we believe that marriage is as much a part of the Faith as baptism. It's not simply a state of life that intersects with our faith: It's a visible sign of the Faith. Marriage is therefore something to be lived out rather than a stagnant and tepid event that establishes a new way to file taxes.

The Catholic Church understands marriage as more than a union between a man and a woman. We believe that marriage is a matrimonial covenant and a great mystery — a living image of the love, absolute and unfailing, that God has for man. Just as God created man out of love, man and woman create out of love. The preaching of Christ and the New Testament also make it clear that marriage bears the mark of the spousal love between Christ and the Church (CCC 1617).

Marriage as a sacrament is unique. It is the only sacrament that is not administered by a minister of the Church. Rather, the man and the woman themselves "mutually confer upon each other the sacrament of Matrimony" (CCC 1623) in the presence of the Church. The celebration of marriage typically takes place in the setting of Holy Mass. Just as Christ offers himself on the altar for his bride, the Church, the new spouses offer their own lives selflessly for each other, uniting themselves to Christ and the paschal mystery.

From the day of marriage, living out a wholesome and loving Catholic marriage brings forth several powerful effects and benefits for souls. When husband and wife are joined together in "one flesh" (Mt 19:5), a bond is formed that is perpetual and exclusive (CCC 1638). This means the marriage is indissoluble and includes only the two spouses. "So they are no longer two but one. What therefore God has joined together, let not man put asunder" (Mt 19:6).

A special and specific grace is communicated to couples. This grace strengthens a couple's commitment to maintaining the marital bond, increasing their love for each other, helping each other attain holiness, and welcoming and educating their children (CCC 1641). The spouses administer this grace, but its source is Christ.

Because marriage is an indissoluble bond and a living sign of Christ's love for us, we are compelled to live our marriages in a way that reflects the dignity of the sacrament. Regarding the bond, spouses must live in unity and with fidelity, giving themselves completely to each other. This might mean weighing the family/work balance, or adopting new habits in handling encounters with the opposite sex.

Spouses bind themselves to remain open to fertility and life. Children are the supreme gift of marriage. Parents are not just the building blocks of society; they are the building blocks of the transmission of the Faith in every generation. Therefore, Catholic parents should be proud that God has entrusted them with the vital work of educating and forming their children according to the precepts and teachings of the Church. This is the reason the family is known as the "domestic church."

Perhaps you are in (or encounter) a marriage in which one spouse is not Catholic, and perhaps has no desire to be. I can identify with this, because I did not enter the Church with my spouse either. If this is your situation, have hope. Chances are good that you didn't think you would ever become a Catholic, either. But God touched your heart and revealed at least some of the fullness of the truth to you. From there, little by little, the scales fell from your eyes. Although I cannot by any means guarantee a conversion, I do have some time-tested steps that might help, whether for your spouse, or for family members and friends:

- Pray that God would communicate himself to your spouse (or family member).

- Ask God, if you are not communicating effectively, to send someone else. Perhaps your loved one needs to hear the truth from a fresh perspective.

- Be patient. It's a requirement for every good relationship, but it is doubly required here, because we cannot convert hearts; only God can do that. Your patience is your visible proof of the peace you have in your new life as a Catholic.

- Set the example. Are you growing in virtue? Are you more engaged in prayer and more focused on your family and kindling your marriage, and perhaps a little less eager for everyone to agree with your decision? Setting a desirable example makes your faith more desirable.

Marriage is an extraordinary sacrament. It is made by your union, but the benefits are directly proportional to your input. Live the fullest marriage possible with the fullness of your newfound faith!

21

Live out your confirmation

The Church has three sacraments of initiation: baptism, confirmation, and the Eucharist. These sacraments bind souls into the Church. While most people are very familiar with baptism and the Eucharist, they know less about confirmation. It's a splendid sacrament that has lifelong effects.

Confirmation is the completion of baptismal graces. As a priest once remarked, if baptism prepared you, confirmation completed you. In this sacrament, Catholics become more perfectly united to Christ. They receive a special strength in the sealing of the Holy Spirit, which prepares them to participate in the missionary role of the Church (CCC 1285). We see this exampled on Easter Sunday and more fully on Pentecost when Christ breathed on the apostles (Jn 20), and later sealed them with the descent the Holy Spirit (Acts 2).

The effects of confirmation are extraordinary. With this sacrament comes the full outpouring of the Holy Spirit. It unites us more firmly to Christ and to the Father, since we are now more deeply united in the graces of baptism. Finally, confirmation enables us to spread and defend the faith by work and action as true witnesses of Christ (CCC 1303). Confirmed Catholics are entrusted with the evangelical mission of the Church. Every Catholic shares in the mission of bringing forth God's kingdom and telling others about Christ and the promises of eternal life. This is how we live out the grace of confirmation.

There are also many fun ways to remember your confirmation and make it part of your daily life. Celebrating the anniversary of your confirmation is a particularly sweet way to memorialize the day you entered into the fullness of Christ's Church. It's likely that you chose a confirmation saint when you were confirmed, and you can seek that saint's intercession each day. Devotion to the Holy Spirit is also a special means of living out the grace particular to the Sacrament of Confirmation. The Holy Spirit is God, the third Person of the Holy Trinity, and we should pray to him. Pray "Come, Holy Spirit" as often as you can, especially when you need the gifts of the Holy Spirit: wisdom, knowledge, understanding, counsel, fortitude, piety, and fear of the Lord.

22

Don't forget the anointing of the sick

The anointing of the sick is an extraordinary sacrament that addresses illness, suffering, and the closeness of death. These moments of life are not foreign concepts to the Catholic Church. Through two millennia of experience and with the inspiration of the Holy Spirit, the Church has much to offer us as we face our own mortality.

In her wisdom, the Church recognizes that illness and suffering can lead even faithful souls to confusion, despair, and revolt against God. But illness, suffering, and the possibility of death also bring opportunities for spiritual maturity, unparalleled self-awareness, and a search for — or a return to — God. Suffering is not purposeless: Even if we can see no good in it, God is using it for a special purpose.

In this vein, we recognize Christ as the physician. Many of the stories in the New Testament are accounts of his healing people and forgiving sins. This is not by mistake: Healing is a primary activity of his ministry, both healing of the body and of the soul. And as Christ gives the Church the ministry of healing the sick in his name (see Mt 10:8; Mk 6:13; Jas 5:14–15), so our priests are prepared to administer an extraordinary sacrament that hopes for our healing. This is the sacrament of the anointing of the sick, also known as the sacrament of the sick or extreme unction.

This sacrament is given to those who are seriously ill. This does not mean that the person must be at the point of death, but if in danger of death from sickness, surgery, or old age, a person may receive the sacrament. This sacrament can be received more than once. Even if the person receives the anointing and his condition worsens, the Church offers multiple applications of the sacrament (CCC 1514–1515).

As with all sacraments, the anointing of the sick is a liturgical celebration, so it includes a number of readings, rites, and prayers. Time permitting, it is preferred that confession with absolution and the Eucharist be received as well. The priest anoints the individual on the forehead and hands with blessed oil while offering a prayer of hope for healing.

One effect of this sacrament is a particular gift of the Holy Spirit, which strengthens and provides peace to overcome suffering with courage. Another effect is that it draws the recipient into closer union with Christ's Passion, consecrating the individual as suffering alongside Christ, producing fruit in the work of redemptive suffering. The sacrament also offers an ecclesial grace that contributes to the good of others and the sanctity of the Church. Finally, the sacrament prepares the person for death as the completion of the anointing sacraments, joining baptism and confirmation as the completion of the Christian life (CCC 1520–1523).

What's imperative for the faithful, then, is to ensure proper care and consideration is given when you or someone else is seriously ill and potentially approaching death. When this happens, make sure to contact your priest and keep him aware of the situation. Also make sure the medical staff understands that you are Catholic and, if the individual is seriously ill, that you would like to consult a priest. Many hospitals also have priests on standby (either close by or in the building) for this specific reason.

23

Attend an ordination

The Rite of Ordination is what "makes" a priest. Because this occurs within the context of the Holy Mass, the faithful are encouraged to attend — all are invited!

Years ago I was invited to an ordination Mass by my confirmation sponsor. I had been a Catholic for only a year at that point, and I had never met any of the men receiving ordination. Despite that, it was a very satisfying experience for me personally.

Principally, I learned more about the priesthood on that day than I ever had before. Each man being ordained had completed years of study in philosophy and theology, as well as discernment, and this gave me confidence in our new clergy. The priesthood was not a last resort for them, or "Plan B" for their lives. Instead, the Church was receiving some of the brightest and most disciplined men the entire region had to offer.

I also learned about the ordination Mass itself. During the liturgy, I watched as the bishop laid hands on each new priest, asking for an invocation of the Holy Spirit to shape them, and anointed their hands with oil to set them apart for their sacred duty. Each of the men being ordained lay prostrate on the floor as a sign of their humility and unworthiness for this new office. Each new priest also received the sacred vestments and vessels that marked the signs of their apostolic ministry: the stole and the chasuble, the chalice, and the paten. All of this gave me a huge appreciation for the priesthood.

After the Mass, I was given a small token by some of the priests: a prayer card marking the day. Even though it was years ago, I still have this card, and when it see it, I say a quick but thoughtful prayer for this priest. Even though I had never met him, and have no idea what happened to him, the bonds of the Church are not separated by distance. I have confidence my prayers for him, and for every priest, are heard by God through Christ who is our High Priest.

If you can, go to an ordination Mass. It's your chance to meet the newest priests in your diocese, offer them your prayers — which they certainly need — and to appreciate the structure of the Church. As an added bonus, there is a plenary indulgence attached to attending an ordination Mass (see section 46 for more on indulgences).

The ordination Mass is not the only opportunity to celebrate with the new priests: You should also seek the schedule and location of a priest's first Mass. This is usually much more personal and endearing, and it often presents the opportunity for the new priest to talk about this vocation. If you get the opportunity, go to an ordination Mass and a priest's first Mass: Out of the hundreds of Masses you will attend in your life, these will remain among the most memorable.

Mary, the
Church, and
the Saints

24

Cultivate a devotion to the Sacred and Immaculate Hearts

If you're a convert, you'll quickly notice that the word "devotion" in the Catholic Church is used somewhat differently than in other religions or denominations. For example, "devotional" to a Protestant usually signifies a book of daily readings or reflections, referring to the time which you "devote" to that particular study, cause, or reading. For Catholics, "devotion" implies a religious practice or prayers focused on a particular aspect of the Faith.

Catholic devotions include a multitude of saints, but there are also specific devotions to Jesus and Mary, often focusing on particular aspects of their identities and relationships with us. One of the most popular of these is devotion to their hearts (yes, literally): the Sacred Heart of Jesus and the Immaculate Heart of Mary. You've probably seen images of the two hearts — the burning heart wrapped in a crown of thorns with a wound in its side, and the fiery heart encircled by roses (and sometimes thorns), pierced by a sword.

Many devotions come from ancient origins, and since the earliest days of Christianity, there has been a general devotion to the Passion of Christ. In the days of the Crusades, as more relics were discovered, veneration grew for the relics that served as tools of Christ's crucifixion — the nails, the crown of thorns, the cross, and the holy shroud (his burial cloth). As the crusaders brought home relics of the Passion along with their newfound zeal, devotions to Jesus' heart also grew, as the bodily center of his personhood as the God-man and the spiritual center of his sufferings for humanity. Various saints, such as Bernard of Clairvaux and Francis of Assisi, carried on this devotion, and in 1353, Pope Innocent VI instituted a Mass honoring the mystery of the Sacred Heart.[3] But it was Saint Margaret Mary Alacoque (1647–1690), a French nun, who established the norms for devotion to the Sacred Heart. This devotion came from Our Lord in a series of visions between 1673 and 1675. If you are interested in learning more about the practice of this devotion, I highly recommend simply reading her autobiography — it will tell you everything you need to know about the saint and the devotion.

Why is devotion to the Sacred Heart so necessary? When we tell someone we love them, we often say that we love them with "all our heart." That's about as much as we can love someone — with that center of our person, with the very thing that keeps us alive, with all our capacity. Well, the same may be said of Jesus, who loves each of us with all his heart. The big difference, of course, is that while we often fail to truly love others with "all our heart," Christ does not. He alone is capable of loving perfectly, as he truly does. We devote ourselves to him to show gratitude, receive hope, and grow in faith and love by remembering how much he loves us. The *Catechism* puts it this way:

> Jesus knew and loved us each and all during his
> life, his agony, and his Passion and gave himself

> up for each one of us: "The Son of God ... loved
> me and gave himself for me." He has loved us all
> with a human heart. For this reason, the Sacred
> Heart of Jesus, pierced by our sins and for our
> salvation, "is quite rightly considered the chief
> sign and symbol of that ... love with which the
> divine Redeemer continually loves the eternal
> Father and all human beings" without excep-
> tion. (478)

Along with Jesus' Sacred Heart, Catholics also practice devotion
to Mary's Immaculate Heart, the very center of her personhood
and of her love for God and for us. Where Jesus' Sacred Heart
is centered on his overwhelmingly perfect love for humanity,
Mary's Immaculate Heart is centered on her immaculate love
(unblemished by any sin or fault) for Jesus and God. Her perfect
love for God leads her to a perfect and complete love for each of
us. While devotion to the Sacred Heart is responsive, a reaction
to his love, devotion to the Immaculate Heart is more emulative,
a desire to imitate Mary's great love for God. Devotees of the
Immaculate Heart focus on Mary's life: her joys, her sorrows, her
obedience, her peace, and her holiness.

It's important to understand both the Sacred and Immaculate Hearts to gain a devotion to them. As human beings, we
were created to be devoted to something. We can see this in very
ordinary, human "devotions" we encounter all around us. Some
people are devoted to collecting baseball cards, others are devoted to their careers, and others are devoted to their families.
It's great to have hobbies, to seek perfection in everything we do,
and to pour ourselves into our relationships; but it is immensely
more important to seek perfection where perfection is: in Jesus'
perfect love for us, and in Mary's complete love for God, and for
us in and through him.

25

Know the approved Marian apparitions

M any people find themselves, even after converting to the Catholic Church, wrestling with the topic of Mary. For myself, though I was reasonably comfortable with the sacraments, the authority of the Church, and the saints, I had not yet worked out Mary's particular importance in salvation history. I was comfortable enough to be Catholic, but it still seemed as though there was an overemphasis on Mary, that Catholics exalted her perhaps a little too much. Marian apparitions made me exceptionally uncomfortable.

Why wouldn't Jesus appear to his followers? Or, in keeping with Scripture, why wouldn't God send an angel to talk to his people instead? After all, is Mary a prophet? Why else would people obey her instructions, act on her warnings, and believe in her revelations?

The Catholic Church acknowledges that the era of public revelation ended with the death of the last apostle, Saint John. Before this, God communicated to his whole people through individuals. When this public revelation died out, so did the obligation to believe in these revelations. Since then, when and if something is revealed to an individual, it falls into the category of private revelation, and it is not binding upon the faith of anyone.

But after reading and reflecting on various Marian apparitions that have occurred throughout history, I began to find it exceedingly fitting that Mary, who is given to us as a spiritual mother (Jn 19:27), would continue to aid, guide, and instruct her children throughout every age. She continues to do as she did at the wedding in Cana, telling us constantly, "Do whatever he tells you" (Jn 2:5). And that's precisely the message we see in those apparitions that have been approved by the Church: Mary encourages us to do the will of her Son, Jesus. In other words, what Mary shares in these private revelations is a call to deepen our adherence to the call of every Christian.

Genuine apparitions and visitations — those which have been investigated and approved by the Church's thorough process — always emphasize an aspect of public revelation. They do not provide unique formulas for getting to heaven or secret recipes for holiness. What's more, Mary never seems to appear to people who are exceptionally spiritual or intellectual, but to good, simple people.

Your level of comfort with apparitions and private revelation should never cause your faith to waver. If someone ever accuses you of imperfect faith because you are not a follower of this or that Marian apparition, remind them that private revelations are just that: private. Still, remember that God can choose to act through other humans, just as he can choose to act outside of nature.

Of course, not all apparitions are of Mary; God frequently sent his angels to encourage individuals or entire communities! Some saints (like Saint Gemma Galgani and Saint Faustina Kowalska) could see their guardian angels, while others (like Saint

Dominic and Saint Joan of Arc) were visited by other saints to support and encourage them in their mission. God ordains these heavenly visitations to broaden faith and to demonstrate his divine will. But without a doubt, the apparitions that continue to garner the most devotion are those of Mary to her children. So without further ado, let's take a look at some of the most important approved Marian apparitions.

OUR LADY OF THE PILLAR

This the earliest recorded apparition of Mary, which occurred around the year A.D. 40. The apostle James had traveled far into Spain to spread the Gospel. One might have expected that James — an eyewitness to the life and ministry of Christ, privileged third apostle of Jesus' inner circle, and an inspired writer of Sacred Scripture — would have no issues evangelizing. But to his dismay and discouragement, he had not made many converts.

Then Mary appeared to him, standing on a pillar and accompanied by angels. She encouraged him, performed some miracles, and encouraged him that he was planting successful seeds of faith. Mary assured James that the faith of those he was evangelizing would be as strong as the pillar she was standing on. As would be the theme in many future apparitions, she requested him to have a chapel built on the site. Today, a glorious church has replaced the original chapel in Zaragoza, Spain. The amazing thing about this apparition is that Mary bilocated, meaning she was in two places at once (a miracle common to some saints during their lifetime). A closer look shows that the apparition at the pillar happened before Mary's assumption into heaven, meaning she was still living in the Holy Land.

OUR LADY OF GUADALUPE

During the sixteenth century, on the hill of Tepayac on the outskirts of modern-day Mexico City, an indigenous man named Juan Diego, who was a devout Catholic, saw Mary. Diego lived in the epicenter of cultural clashes between the Aztecs and the Spanish. The native Aztecs insisted on the validity of their cultural traditions and wisdom, while the Spaniards insisted on the truths of Christianity.

In her apparition, Mary asked Juan Diego to build a church, but his bishop rejected the suggestion. She asked again, instructing Diego to be more persistent, and the bishop requested a physical sign to assure the identity of the woman supposedly appearing. Juan Diego brought back, at Mary's bidding, a cloak-full of out-of-season roses. He carried them in his *tilma*, which he wore in keeping with the general custom of that time and place. The bishop was astonished, not as much for the roses as the image that appeared when they fell. There, on Diego's *tilma*, was a masterpiece of incredible detail and brilliance: the image today commonly known as Our Lady of Guadalupe.

The uniqueness of the image astonished both Aztecs and Spaniards. The image on the *tilma* contains symbols from Aztec culture and belief to illuminate Mary's identity. The blue-green mantle was the color reserved for the divine couple Ometecuhtli and Omecihuatl; the Virgin's belt was a traditional sign of pregnancy — an allusion to the Incarnation. The Aztecs would interpret the rays of the sun radiating from her image to mean that she is above even their sun god, but her hands praying signify that there is still one greater than her. From the layout of the stars on her cloak to the moon she is standing on, the religious iconography is meaningful to both Christians and the indigenous peoples. The Aztecs believed that their sacrifices to the gods of the sun and stars would save them, but they were shown how the sacrifice of the One who *made* the sun and the stars was the ultimate appropriation for our sins. The apparition of Our Lady of Guadalupe influenced over ten million conversions in under ten years. She is still beloved throughout the Americas.

OUR LADY OF THE MIRACULOUS MEDAL

Aside from a crucifix, the Miraculous Medal is perhaps the most-worn item of Catholic devotion in the world. It comes from a nineteenth-century apparition of Our Lady to a French novice in the Daughters of Charity named Catherine Labouré. In 1830, Our Lady appeared to Catherine and asked her to make a medallion in a design representing the apparition. It was two years later when Catherine's priest took the information to the archbishop, who approved of the design and production. After many miracles and graces, it became known as the Miraculous Medal, just as Mary had promised Catherine.

It is important to note that the timing of Mary's apparitions is always relevant: This one came during the July Revolution, when France was again turned upside down with turmoil, confusion, and religious inequality and persecutions. Our Lady appeared to show support and care for her people, as well as a means of miracles when many Catholics were praying for one.

OUR LADY OF LOURDES

An uncatechized fourteen-year-old might be a confusing choice for a Marian apparition, but God chooses the lowly (1 Cor 1:28). Mary appeared to little Bernadette Soubirous in Lourdes, France, in 1858, but the uneducated girl did not recognize her. She knew her only as a beautiful lady. Mary appeared to Bernadette multiple times in a lowly grotto. Civil authorities fenced off the site while Church authorities debated the truth of Bernadette's vision. When the barricade was lifted, Bernadette returned and was told by the mysterious lady, "I am the Immaculate Conception."

Less than four years earlier, in an apostolic constitution, Pope Pius IX had defined the dogma of the Immaculate Conception, which states that Mary was born without original sin.[4]

Bernadette, a poor, uneducated girl, was unfamiliar with the theological debate. Years later, the apparition received ecclesial approval. Since then, Lourdes has been one of the most popular pilgrimage sites in the world. Some seven thousand people have reported miracles, and of them, sixty-nine have endured the arduous process of approval.

OUR LADY OF FÁTIMA

Arguably the most important apparition in modern times, the visions at Fátima impacted almost the entire twentieth century. Three shepherd children were visited by Mary in the fields near Fátima in Portugal. Word spread quickly about the place and time (indicated by Mary) where the children would receive future visions, and some seventy thousand were in attendance to witness the last prophesied appearance in October 1917. From there, they reported the Miracle of the Sun, in which the sun seemed to dance in the sky, changing shape, color, and distance from the earth.

To the children, Mary delivered a special message: She asked them to promote peace through praying the Rosary and making sacrifices. The children also received three specific messages, which they were to keep secret for a time, about events that would unfold over the next several decades. The "secrets" were eventually disclosed to clerical authorities and publicized later, by which point many years had passed. These included a terrifying vision of hell, the Second World War, errors of Russian atheism and religious persecution, the attempted assassination of Pope John Paul II in 1981, the consecration of Russia, and more.

26
Pray to the saints

The saints — holy men and women who we are confident are in heaven — are prime examples of Catholics who triumphed in their faith. While they are models of holiness, they are also shockingly relatable. Saints Benedict and Aloysius Gonzaga both practiced penance and mortification to maintain purity. Saint Thérèse of Lisieux battled anxiety. And nearly all of the apostles ran away when Jesus was arrested and killed; yet they returned to receive the Holy Spirit and share the Gospel with the world. Despite their shortcomings, the saints accomplished the impossible. The weakest of them became the greatest, and the ones who led private and quiet lives were eventually heard throughout the world.

Following others is a choice. When we choose to follow the saints, that choice shapes who we are and the choices we make. We may follow a hundred or so people online, and we may have even more friends elsewhere; but, in proportion, is the time we spend with the saints as much as it ought to be? Following the saints involves getting to know them beyond the facts on their Wikipedia page. It means reading their writings, praying to them, and asking them to teach us to think like them, talk like them, and act like them.

Yes, we can be friends with the saints! This isn't just a weird Catholic practice, but a deeply human reality. Humans want to believe in the afterlife, and every culture shares an idea that those who have gone before us — especially our heroes — are looking after us. At the same time, it is important to note this difference: Christians do not honor the saints as some form of ancestor or idol worship. This would be contrary to the first commandment: "You shall have no other gods before me. You shall not make for yourself a graven image, or any likeness of anything that is in heaven above, or that is in the earth beneath, or that is in the water under the earth; you shall not bow down to them or serve them" (Ex 20:3–5). We do not adore the saints in worship but venerate them as our champions and examples, and ask for their help since they won the battles we still face.

Also, we definitely do not pray to the saints alone, as if we believe they are the ones blessing us or performing miracles. The Bible reminds us that "the prayer of a righteous man has great power in its effects" (Jas 5:16). Those who are most righteous, living in the presence of God in heaven, are the most effective intercessors on our behalf with God, the one mediator. Indeed, we can ask our friends on earth to pray for us, but we have more cause to ask our friends in heaven for prayers.

The *Dogmatic Constitution on the Church* puts it like this: "For after they have been received into their heavenly home and are present to the Lord ... they do not cease to intercede with the Father for us, showing forth the merits which they won on earth through the one Mediator between God and man, serving God in all things and filling up in their flesh those things which are lacking of the sufferings of Christ for his body which is the Church. Thus by their brotherly interest our weakness is greatly strengthened."[5] What it boils down to is that the communion of saints is the Church. We are held together in Christ, and we build each other up in holiness and in love.

But there is still that nagging question about the difference between having a mediator and having intercessors. To be an intercessor means to go or come between two parties, to plead before one of them on behalf of the other. Praying to the saints is the same as your friend coming to you and saying, "My mother is gravely ill; will you pray for her?" When we pray for others on earth, we intercede with God for the intentions of the other person. A mediator, though, is a person who joins together two estranged parties. Jesus, by his salvific work on Calvary, brings us into communion with God as children, inheritors of the kingdom of heaven. The saints are intercessors; Jesus alone is our mediator with God.

Another common objection against praying to the saints and angels is that they cannot possibly listen to hundreds of prayers at once because they are not omniscient as is God; it would be like listening to a crowd of people talking at the same time. But that question is based on the assumption that the restrictions of earth are the restrictions of heaven. In heaven, the saints participate in the divine essence of God through the beatific vision. To make matters less complicated, we believe that "those in heaven have an insight of God's glory," as Thomas Aquinas puts it,[6] and therefore, they have knowledge that that glory encompasses the petitions of the Church on earth. The best summary I've ever heard was actually from a Protestant pastor, who said of his recently deceased son, "If Jesus can hear me and he is united with Jesus, then my son can hear me."

In heaven, there is no time; there is only forever. Remember, the saints live in perfection of love. On earth, it is our Spirit-led desire to pray for others to will good for them, but we often fail by forgetting to pray and falling asleep, as the apostles did in Gethsemane. In heaven, that holy desire to pray for our benefit is perfected in the completeness of God's love, and the saints never forget or fall asleep.

Some see the intercession of the saints as perhaps aiming too low, since we can go directly to God with our prayers. The answer is simple: We ought to pray to God about everything each time we pray, without exception. Though this is true, asking others to pray for us as well is a mark of Christianity. Paul tells the Romans, "I appeal to you … to strive together with me in your prayers to God on my behalf" (Rom 15:30), and elsewhere (see also Rom 15:30–32, Eph 6:18–20, Col 4:3, 1 Thes 5:25, 2 Thes 1:1, 2 Thes 3:1). Most fundamentally, Jesus requires that we pray for others, and not only for those who ask us to do so (Mt 5:44). If we follow this command, even if imperfectly, how much more will the saints in heaven, who always do God's will, continue to do as Jesus commanded in praying for us.

27

Get to know some saints

Open your recent call list on your phone, and you'll quickly notice you see the same names over and over. You can further sort your contacts by name, by frequency, by recency, and so on. Go to your favorite messaging app, and you'll see something similar. You can sort these similarly, but sorting only gets you so far. Finding that person who said that one thing, or sent you that one link, did that favor for you, or who was the one you promised you'd get back to — there's no way to sort for those. That only comes by memory.

The saints are the same. You'll do good to remember the ones you can count on in times of joy, in times of need, and in times where you just need that special charism. These are patron saints. These saints are the advocate of an activity or a state of life or place, or really anything. There are patrons of science and youth, patrons of dog trainers and parishes. There are even patron saints of entire countries and causes (like suffering from cancer). Patrons become so through many customs or events, but usually involve a similitude to their life on earth or miracles for which they have been petitioned. Saints like …

SAINT ANTHONY OF PADUA

"Where are my keys?!"

Saint Anthony of Padua is the patron saint of lost things. How did he get that patronage? One story goes that a novice stole his book and fled the monastery, but after Anthony prayed fervently, the novice returned it and came back to the monastery. Anthony was the "hammer to heretics," and he showed an intense and undying love for those who were lost — grave sinners and unbelievers. Catholics have counted on him to find their lost objects since the thirteenth century.

SAINT FRANCIS OF ASSISI

Have a pet? You can have them blessed on October 4, Saint Francis of Assisi's feast day. Saint Francis reminds us how all creatures point back to God, their Creator.

SAINT JOSEPH

Do you have a job? Need a job? Count on the intercession of Saint Joseph, Christ's foster father and the patron of laborers, to aid you. Appropriately, he's also the patron saint of fathers.

SAINT MICHAEL THE ARCHANGEL

Saint Michael is the great defender of believers, ready and able to take on the most intense and hellish spiritual battles on our behalf. Never hesitate to say the Prayer of Saint Michael the Archangel. Are you or is someone you know a police officer or a soldier? You may both rely on the intercessions of Saint Michael the Archangel to defend you and help you serve honorably.

SAINT MONICA

All mothers can learn from and be comforted by the life of Saint Monica. She was the mother of Saint Augustine, for whom she prayed endlessly until his conversion.

There are many more: patrons of youth, nightmares, comedians, students, widows, and nearly everything else you can think of. Keep the saints on speed dial to know who to go to throughout your life, and continue to discover new saints throughout the liturgical year.

Excellent resources to learn more about the saints include Butler's *Lives of the Saints* and *The Book of Saints* by Basil Watkins.

28
Go on a pilgrimage

Humans of every culture and religion have always visited holy places, whether to pay homage, fulfill a vow, or beg for divine intervention. The oldest and most revered pilgrimage for Christians is, of course, the Holy Land, but there are many other incredible destinations.

We should note that making a pilgrimage is not the same as taking a vacation. Pilgrimages can also be times of relaxation, but they are not opportunities to splurge, be pampered, or purchase frivolous entertainment. Pilgrimages require a mix of sacrifice, silence, humility, contemplation, and prayer. If you put your desires aside for just a few days and allow yourself to be more available to the wisdom of the Holy Spirit, you can turn nearly any adventure into a pilgrimage.

GO HOME TO ROME
The City of Love, the City on Seven Hills, the City of God, the *Caput Mundi* (Capital of the World), *Urbus Sacra* (Sacred City), the Eternal City ... Rome has many names.

From a secular standpoint, Rome is fascinating for its age and its far-reaching impact. Visit the most ancient ruins of the oldest cities in Europe, and you'll find Roman roads and the remains of Roman buildings. When the rest of the Western world was trying to understand why seeds don't grow in poor soil and figuring out a good use for the horse, the Romans were writing poetry, conquering everything in sight just for the heck of it, and literally giving other civilizations language, education, and health care just to expand their economy and have someone to trade with.

From a Catholic standpoint, Rome has an even greater draw. It is a destination, not just for historical exploration, but for pilgrimage. The heritage of Rome is the heritage of the martyrs, as thousands of Christian martyrs nourished the foundation of the Church, beginning in Rome. As Tertullian famously expressed it, "The blood of the martyrs is the seed of the Church."

As a pilgrim to Rome, you certainly won't be bored. Rome is home to about nine hundred churches. Pilgrims should plan to visit the four major basilicas — Saint Peter's, Saint Paul Outside the Walls, Saint Mary Major, and Saint John Lateran — and the seven pilgrimage churches, a route many of the saints took. These visits will require a few hours of walking, but they are well worth it. You can also visit the Vatican City State, home of the pope. On Sundays, pilgrims can see the pope and say the Angelus with him. Take time to wander the city a bit, too. You'll be awestruck when you stumble into a random church where a saint, an incorruptible, or the buried relic of an apostle is located. Oh, and you'll enjoy the food, too. Go to Rome as soon and as often as possible, and when you get there, please pray for me.

TRAVEL THE WORLD

Many Catholics also make pilgrimages to places where great miracles or apparitions (or both) have occurred: Lourdes, France; Guadalupe, Mexico; Turin, Italy; and even Champion, Wisconsin, where Our Lady appeared. All are popular destinations for pilgrims. Finally — and this is somewhat of a catchall — many beautiful pilgrimages are made to places where important historical events in the Church have taken place. You might decide to visit Montepulciano, Italy, birthplace of numerous saints, popes, cardinals, and bishops, such as Robert Bellarmine, Agnes, and Pope Marcellus II. Or you could take a trip to the enormous Christ the Redeemer statue in Rio de Janeiro, Brazil. Each of these makes for an adventure and an opportunity to become filled with the Holy Spirit, rejuvenated to take up new vows and renew old ones.

I once took a four-day pilgrimage to the city of Nagasaki, Japan. This city is the gateway of the Christian faith in the Far East. The Christians of Japan suffered dramatic persecutions for four hundred years, and Nagasaki was the site of many martyrdoms. The city is home to Nishizaka Hill, where Paul Miki and his twenty-five companions died for the Faith in 1597, as well as the famous 188 martyrs in the seventeenth century. Nagasaki is also the site where hundreds of thousands perished in the Second World War. When the atomic bomb exploded just five hundred meters from the Urakami Cathedral, it destroyed the site and leveled the area. But in the ashes and plumes was found the head of a statue of Mary, which is now carried year after year through the streets in a procession. This head is a unique symbol of the faith of the Christians in Nagasaki: able to endure anything.

OR STAY CLOSER TO HOME

But you don't need to go to Europe or Nagasaki to have a great pilgrimage. You'll be surprised to find out how many unique and beautiful destinations of the Faith don't require leaving the United States. Spanish missions dot the West Coast. Montana is home to one of the largest Marian statues in the world. Omaha, Nebraska, and St. Louis, Missouri, have cathedrals that rival the beautiful churches of Rome. Washington, D.C., boasts one of the largest basilicas in the world, and Montreal has one of the most ornate. There are shrines to many saints and to Our Lady around the country. Look around your diocese or state for local pilgrimage opportunities. You don't have to go far: The pilgrimage is in the destination and the journey itself. Whether it's the Via Francigena, the ancient world's most famous pilgrim route to Rome, or a trip to your local cathedral, you can have the same result: a new appreciation for our faith and a renewed trust, confidence, and desire to serve God.

29

Consider joining
a Third Order

Few Catholics know what a third order is, even those who were raised in the Church. The third orders are secular branches of the established religious orders, such as the Franciscans, the Carmelites, and the Dominicans. These orders include priests and nuns, of course, but many of them also have a third order, which is made up of laypeople. There are significant benefits to joining the third order, and it's worth spending some time learning about them and discerning whether or not you are called to join one.

The primary benefits of joining a third order are spiritual direction and discipline, which come by meeting regularly with members of a local chapter (or other designation), participating in the spiritual exercises central to the order, working toward a joint mission in the local community, and learning from the wisdom and example of the order's saints. Furthermore, the third order helps instill discipline through accountability and a stricter routine of prayer and devotion.

Each order possesses a particular charism. The Dominicans

are the Order of Preachers, so they typically focus on community outreach through teaching and personal study. Aside from their founder and patron, Saint Dominic, their influences come from saints like Thomas Aquinas, Catherine of Siena, and many others. Third Order Franciscans are influenced by the traditions of Saint Francis of Assisi, as well as others such as Clare of Assisi, Anthony of Padua, and Padre Pio. They focus on humility and service to the poor. Third Order Carmelites, similarly, follow in the general tradition of their order's saints, such as Teresa of Ávila and John of the Cross, often living out a more arduous spirituality of deep contemplation.

Third order participants are separated into two groups: regulars (or religious), who live in communities and take vows, and seculars, who live in the world and make solemn promises. Both offer enriching and unique opportunities for Catholics who have families, careers, and other responsibilities in the world to grow closer to Christ and grow in love by serving others. To learn more, talk to folks within your diocese, or use an internet search to see what orders offer chapters near your location.

30

Adorn your home with religious articles

If you haven't already, consider making adjustments to the décor in your house to reflect the faith you profess and enjoy. This idea was brought up to me when I first had my house blessed. My priest, Father Stillmunks, knew I was a new convert, so he brought over a crucifix.

He said, "You have a crucifix, right?"

"Yes, Father."

"Well I want you to have this one, too. Put it in a special place. Try to outfit your home so that no matter where you look, you have the Faith in front of you."

It's no secret that Catholics have a special tradition of visually expressing their faith, whether it is with a Marian statue in their yard or a crucifix in every room. We decorate our homes with religious objects not only as a matter of taste and fashion, but as a mode of inspiration and sanctification.

So I encourage you to adorn your house with holy items so that every room is a place where the Faith is visually present. I can witness that this is a sure means of sanctifying your household and will help you in moments of joy and of grief. There have been times when I have been upset with my children, and as I turn around ready to throw my hands in the air, I see a depiction of Joseph tenderly guiding Jesus to become a master carpenter. The image reminds me of the patience needed in a faithful father. My wife talks of a time when she had had it "up to here" with the kids, and right in front of her was a borrowed relic of Saint Monica, patron of mothers. When we have guests over, the shadow box of baptism candles on the wall always opens a conversation about the Catholic Faith.

If you don't yet have any religious articles in your house, I suggest you begin with a crucifix. Being reminded of the Passion of Christ and his immeasurable love for us is the most excellent symbol Catholics can display in their houses. I also recommend a holy water font at the entrance to your home. Grab a small bottle to hold holy water from your parish and keep the bowl full. Whether coming or going, dip your finger in and make the Sign of the Cross. This is a powerful and practical means of preparing for spiritual battle. Here are some other solid suggestions:

- A holy image or icon of Mary, the Trinity, angels, the Holy Family, or the saints
- Statues of Jesus, Mary, and the saints
- An image of the pope (current or past)
- A large wall-mounted Rosary
- Garden statues
- Prayer candles (beeswax is a Catholic favorite)
- Items from a baptism (christening gown, candle, etc.)

Whether it's a simple saint card on the bathroom mirror or an authentic mosaic from Ravenna, these articles of religious art and expression will bless your house for years to come. Find these and other items at your local Catholic bookstore or in one of the numerous Catholic stores online.

31

Start a holy card collection

My brother started collecting baseball cards as a child. By the time he was fifteen or sixteen years old, he had around eleven thousand cards, including a few unique specimens. He still has the cards in a closet somewhere. They might be gathering dust, but he retains a memory for the players, the stats, the stories, and the career milestones. My brother can rattle off the yardage of the longest home run ever hit and the whole story behind it. He can tell me, without hesitation, how many RBIs a player had in a career, all because he enjoyed the simple hobby of collecting cards.

There's a special card-collecting tradition among Catholics. They go by many names: holy cards, prayer cards, saint cards, Mass cards. The tradition goes way back to the thirteenth century, to the popularity of woodcuts. These were an inexpensive means of collecting art, and most woodcuts were of a holy image — usually a saint or an image of the Passion of Christ. The oldest known surviving woodcut is of Saint Christopher, dated around 1423, and there are many others. As technology advanced, printed cards became a popular and affordable article of religious devotion. Today, there are many kinds and versions of holy cards.

They have many benefits. First, their imagery inspires our faith. Who looks at a picture of a family member and isn't thrilled with joy or touched with memories? And what kid isn't inspired to be the best when he looks at a picture of his sports hero? The same goes for holy cards: They boost our faith and joy with the image of something sacred or spiritual. They're usually used for prayer, though some don't have any inscriptions.

Like collecting sports cards, collecting holy cards can bring knowledge and experience. Knowledge and experience inform our faith, and when our faith grows, we grow closer to Christ. If done with prayerful purpose, not merely as a hoarding habit, collecting saint cards can be a serious benefit to your soul.

You can get saint cards at any Catholic bookstore, and your parish likely prints them for some events, too. It's common for priests to print hundreds of prayer cards for their ordination — it guarantees much-needed prayers. At a Catholic funeral the family will often distribute prayer cards as a reminder to pray for the soul of the deceased. You can make your own, too. The coolest way I've ever received a prayer card is when I buy old Catholic books, either from antique stores or online sources. With proven success, I almost always get a really old prayer card. (And they just don't make them like they used to).

Carry them in your wallet. Stick them in your mirror to remember to pray in the morning. Use them in your cubicle. Laminate them, punch a hole in the corner, and make a ring of cards for your toddler to look through. Use them as bookmarks. Give them away in greeting cards or with books you buy as gifts. Keep one in your pocket or your planner. Or get a binder and stick the cards in the card slots used for sports cards. Pick a card, any card — you can't go wrong.

Prayer

32

Make the Sign of the Cross

Like the early Christians, we still make the Sign of the Cross. It is not just the opening of a prayer; it is its own prayer. The Sign of the Cross brings Christ's sacrifice, the basis of our faith, into whatever we are praying about, concerned with, or struggling over. When we pray, or do anything, "in the name of the Father, and of the Son, and of the Holy Spirit," we are consecrating that action to the Trinity, and all the mystery and truth that go with it. As Catholics, we make the Sign of the Cross so often that it can become just muscle memory, but we should make this a real prayer, saying it with faith and confidence every time.

There are multiple ways we can make the Sign of the Cross. Most common is the tracing of two lines from forehead to breast, and shoulder to shoulder, using our right hand. We do this at the start and end of Mass, and before most prayers. The little Sign of the Cross is when we use our thumb (sometimes another finger) to trace a cross, usually over the forehead as on Ash Wednesday and when a person is baptized. At the announcement of the Gospel reading in Mass, we make the little cross over our forehead, lips, and breast. Bishops and priests will also make a Sign of the Cross with one hand as they bless different objects or people, as in the benediction concluding Mass.

The *Catholic Encyclopedia* suggests that the Sign of the Cross is a tradition from patristic literature on the Old Testament, where God's people would trace a "tau" on their forehead (Ex 9:4). It finds its fulfilled meaning in Christianity as we identify with the Passion of the Savior. Tertullian, who wrote in the second century, records that Christians traced a small cross on their heads "at every forward step and movement, at every going in and out, when we put on our clothes and shoes, when we bathe, when we sit at table, when we light the lamps, on couch, on seat, in all the ordinary actions of daily life, we trace upon the forehead the sign."[7] Saint Cyril of Jerusalem, Church Father of the fourth century, also witnesses to the use of the Sign: "Be the Cross our seal made with boldness by our fingers on our brow, and on everything; over the bread we eat, and the cups we drink; in our comings in, and goings out; before our sleep, when we lie down and when we rise up; when we are in the way, and when we are still. ... It is the Sign of the faithful."[8] That the sign of the cross is of early origin is undeniable.

The Sign of the Cross should be considered one of the premier symbols of the Catholic Church. Why the cross? I enjoy the words of James Cardinal Gibbons: "The cross is held in the highest reverence by Catholics, because it was the instrument of our Savior's crucifixion. It surmounts our churches and adorns our sanctuaries. We venerate it as the emblem of our salvation."[9]

It's not superstition that drives Catholics to make the Sign early and often. It is principally a prayer, and in this prayer we identify ourselves with our crucified Savior, sanctify ourselves and whatever we intend to bless in the name of the Trinity, and invoke the power of God's holy name. Making the Sign of the Cross does several other things as well: We profess our faith, affirm the reality of the Trinity, open ourselves to grace, and reaffirm our baptism. Another special effect of the sign is that it is a sure prayer of exorcism. Cyril called it "the dread of devils."[10]

With this in mind, when should you make the Sign? I say, if it's important, sanctify it. Make the Sign in hope, or in thanksgiving. Besides liturgically and when dipping your fingers in holy water, you might make the Sign of the Cross especially when you pass a Church, see a holy image, pass a cemetery, when someone says they are praying for you, when you're afraid, and when your friends online ask for prayers.

33

Pray daily

Daily prayer is a requirement of every Christian, and though life is busy, Catholics who are serious about their spiritual state must consider daily prayer their number one priority. There are several ways to accomplish this, and keep in mind that different forms of prayer will work for different stages in your life. Your first priority should be to pray with love and attention, no matter how much time you set aside.

First, begin each morning with the Sign of the Cross at least. The first moment in your day is the best moment of the day to acknowledge God, offer him your day with a short prayer, and ask him to guide your path. Sometime in your morning routine, consider the words of the Psalmist, "Your word is a lamp unto my feet" (Ps 119:105), and read a short passage from a spiritual book, a devotional, or right from your Bible. Make this routine your "morning offering" and do the same at night before bed.

As Christians, we are all called to develop the attitude urged by Saint Paul, "Pray at all times in the Spirit, with all prayer and supplication. To that end keep alert with all perseverance, making supplication for all the saints" (Eph 6:18). I find it helpful to focus on the idea of keeping alert. The word in Greek, *agrypneō*, means to be watchful, attentive, and ready. What Paul is telling us here is not to sit in a pew and keep perfect posture with every moment we are awake, but to be prayerful in our day, aware of the presence and love of God. We can be prayerful in our meals by being considerate of our body as a temple and eating moderately. We can be prayerful in our profession by seeking to work with a Christian ethos and to glorify God. We can be prayerful in our relaxation and leisure by being grateful, enjoying peace, and sharing our joy with others.

Finally, although it is monumentally important to make the other two suggestions regular habits, we must also take the time to make a more focused prayer. I suggest making a goal of twenty minutes per day, set aside as a time for God alone, with no distractions. Start with five or ten minutes, setting a timer so you don't have to keep checking the clock. During this time, talk to God about your day. Pray for your needs and those of others. Pray for the intercession of the saints. Make sure to spend an adequate amount of time in personal prayer, but be sure also to include some of this time praying with your spouse and kids as one family. Lastly, give yourself a period of silence to hear what God is telling you. The earth probably won't tremble, and your skin probably won't get goosebumps (though these things might happen), but you will, with practice in listening, hear God's voice directing your life.

Beginning a habit of daily prayer does not have to be overwhelming. It takes just a few simple steps: Wake up and go to sleep with a God-filled thought and short prayer, acknowledge God in your work and routine, and take just twenty minutes to seek his counsel and express your gratitude.

34
Pray with your family

Because it's such an important topic, I need to explain more about praying with your family. Of course, it's essential to pray for your family, but it's exceptionally more important to *pray with them*. It's not just important; it's imperative. Your children and your spouse absolutely need you present (and active) during prayer time.

I admit, I am a massive introvert when it comes to prayer. I really prefer to find quiet places for my prayer time. This is not bad, but unchecked it led to years of not intentionally praying with my children, or even with my spouse as much as I should have. Though I prayed morning and evening prayers from the full Divine Office, and although I knew it was wholesome to "pray in secret," it took me a while to realize just how vital my presence and example are in guiding and influencing members of my family.

A chaplain of mine woke me up when he remarked that family prayer is more than the seventeen seconds we pray before mealtime. The fact is, children look to you, mom or dad, to show them *what* prayer is, *where* to pray, *when* praying is appropriate, *whom* we pray with and for, *how* we pray, and of course *why* we pray at all. Your kids are paying attention, even at mealtime prayer, no matter how focused they seem to be on avoiding the asparagus.

You don't need to be intimidated: Start small. In the morning at some point, and without exception before bedtime, pray as a family. You can use a small set of well-known prayers. My family gathers after all eighty teeth have been brushed, and at a minimum we pray one Our Father, three Hail Marys, a Glory Be, the "Now I Lay Me Down to Sleep" prayer, a short litany of blessing for all immediate family and godparents; and we invite the kids to also pray a short personal prayer.

That might seem like a lot, but it takes three to five minutes, perfect for children under ten. The repetition forms a basis for the children to pray on their own. Not to mention, it has practical benefits: It winds them down and more noticeably cues them in on bedtime. By ending the day in a joyful and calming prayer, they collect themselves much better than before, and the routine — which kids love — helps establish a habit of prayer. In fact, there are often nights in which one of my petitions led me to let them pray more Hail Marys (and that I never refuse).

A similar, and perhaps briefer, routine can happen in the morning. If not right after they wake up, it can be after teeth are brushed or on the way to school in the car. If your kids are older, shape up these prayer times as they mature. Consider praying a decade of the Rosary, or even the full thing, as a family, and give your kids some moments to pray, reflect, or meditate in front of an icon or statue by themselves.

Another invaluable tool I always recommend is a journal. We use it to jot down prayers from everyone in our family (even our toddlers). It's a good way to help keep kids on track, and to demonstrate progression in their spiritual life and habits. Actually, this is where the fun really happens, because kids often pray the most ridiculous and sidesplitting prayers. From losing more teeth to having another birthday the next day, they're sure to make you want to record their requests. Remind them about it weeks or years later, and it'll cement the continuity of joy in prayer in their minds. Children are also capable of some of the most honest and heartfelt prayers you'll ever hear. One time, one of my sons asked for nothing more than for his brother to do well in school after he overheard a series of stern discussions involving grades and behavior. Another time, after praying the same basic prayer for weeks and appearing uninterested, my oldest gave a solemn thanks for having "such a beautiful sister." Even if it feels mundane, journal about it. In moments when your kids are scared of the closet or in need of healing, they can go back to the prayer journals to remember how faithful God has been.

Don't ever forget to pray with your spouse. Remember that the two of you — not your priest, deacon, or anyone else — are the ministers of this sacrament. You are formed together in one flesh for the purpose of helping each other (and your children, if you are so blessed) get to heaven. Even if it feels weird at first and even after ten tries, do it. You might be exhausted from work, but do it anyway. And even if your favorite show to watch together is on in a few minutes, stop what you are doing and give yourself some perspective: Couples need communication, and prayer is the deepest and most impactful form. Maybe you can do both — or maybe praying should take precedence over watching television tonight.

35

Prepare a prayer corner

As I've gotten older as a Catholic and studied the lives of holy people, ancient and modern, I've realized that their lives each contain a common strategy for self-composition and closeness to the Lord: alone time. More importantly, this "alone time" wasn't alone at all; it was time spent with the Lord. To make prayer time a real habit in your life, I highly recommend setting aside a designated space for it in your house.

This space doesn't need to be a full room. It can be just a small corner. The setup is simple: get a chair and a small table or stand, and add a few items that can help bring you into a moment to be closer with the Lord. Many people add visual aids, such as prayer cards, a crucifix, a statue of a favorite saint or angel, and a candle. The visuals help with concentration, placing before us the lives of the saints and the sacrifice of Our Lord. In a designated prayer corner, your prayer can be as simple as the silence of contemplation.

Your prayer corner can also be interactive. You could get a spiritual book you enjoy and keep it there to read a few pages when you sit down to focus on your spiritual life. Another great idea is to keep a journal on hand to jot down your thoughts, prayers, emotions, and hopes.

Of course, while the visual stimulants are inspiring, and the interactive devices are engaging, the prayer corner should be, above all, about prayer. Make sure yours has a solid Catholic book of prayers, maybe a missalette with the daily Mass readings, and definitely a Rosary. Pray however you need to, but always pray, and pray always.

God, like our parents, knows we need many moments to collect ourselves. At the end of a stressful week, or after we exchange harsh words with our spouse, we need to seek out the solution that has always worked: prayer, by ourselves. So whenever we need some alone time or a restful moment, we should put ourselves in the prayer corner. When our kids are acting out, we can send them to the prayer corner, too. Kids and adults alike need this time to stop, relax, and invite the Lord into our lives.

36

Learn to pray the Rosary

I highly encourage you to learn to pray the Rosary. This beautiful prayer is a union of the Gospel and intercessory petition. Popes and saints recommend the Rosary not only for growth in virtues, but for winning astonishing victories and defeating heresy.

In the "Hail Mary," we honor Mary as the Second Eve, who together with her Son, Jesus, fulfilled the first prophecy in the Bible. After Adam and Eve fell into temptation, God told Eve, "I will put enmity between you and the woman, and between your offspring and hers; he will strike your head, and you will strike his heel" (Gn 3:15). The completion of this short verse began when Mary accepted her role as the bearer of the Messiah, and it was fully completed when Christ conquered sin by his death and Resurrection. In the Rosary, we repeat and contemplate this incredible mystery.

Catholics pray the Rosary because it draws us closer to Jesus, and because it is a powerful prayer for obtaining graces, healing, and divine help. Many saints had a deep devotion to the Rosary. Here are some of my favorite quotes from saints and other historical figures on this beautiful prayer:

- "If you want to reach these hardened souls and win them over to God, preach my Rosary." — Our Lady to Saint Dominic
- "The greatest method of praying is to pray the Rosary." — Saint Francis de Sales
- "It was not courage, not arms, not leaders, but Mary of the Rosary that made us victors." — Venetian Senators after the Battle of Lepanto
- "When the holy Rosary is said well, it gives Jesus and Mary more glory and is more meritorious than any other prayer." — Saint Louis de Montfort
- "If I had an army to say the Rosary, I could conquer the world." — Blessed Pope Pius IX
- "The Rosary is the most excellent form of prayer and the most efficacious means of attaining eternal life. It is the remedy for all our evils, the root of all our blessings. There is no more excellent way of praying." — Pope Leo XIII
- "Pray very much the prayers of the Rosary. I alone am able to save you from the calamities." — Mary in Akita, Japan, "The Rosary is the weapon." — Saint Padre Pio
- "The Rosary is a prayer both so humble and simple and theologically rich in Biblical content. I beg you to pray it." — Pope Saint John Paul II

The Rosary combines history and our belief in the hope of the Resurrection. It further includes the prayer given to us by Jesus in the Our Father, and four sets of mysteries of the Faith, through which we contemplate the life, ministry, and Passion of our Lord: the Joyful, Luminous, Sorrowful, and Glorious Mysteries. Learning the Rosary and making a habit of praying it will equip you for spiritual combat and help you grow in holiness.

37

Practice mortification

As you begin to take baby steps in the spiritual life, you'll find yourself looking for the best ways to take longer strides toward holiness. Besides fervent prayer and joyful almsgiving, the Church encourages a third key to the spiritual life: fasting and self-mortification. Scripture and the saints concur that this is a very important part of growing in holiness.

Here are just a few helpful quotes about the efficacy of mortification:

- Proverbs 20:30: "Blows that wound cleanse away evil; strokes make clean the innermost parts."
- Saint Paul: "I pommel my body and subdue it, lest after preaching to others I myself should be disqualified" (1 Cor 9:27). ("Pommel" literally means to beat or strike physically.)
- Saint Aloysius Gonzaga: "I am a crooked piece of iron, and have come into religion to be made straight by the hammer of mortification and penance."
- Saint Philip Neri: "Where there is no great mor-

tification there is no great sanctity."

All the saints practiced mortification to various degrees, as the Holy Spirit inspired them. Some of the greats include Peter Damien, Jane Frances de Chantal, Alphonsus Liguori, Gemma Galgani, Francis de Sales, and John of the Cross. That said, mortification is an "advanced" technique in the spiritual toolkit. As a new Catholic, I recommend acquainting yourself with the requirements the Church sets forth for abstinence and fasting. The United States Conference of Catholic Bishops (USCCB) has determined that Ash Wednesday and Good Friday are obligatory days of fasting and abstinence for Catholics. In addition to these, all Fridays during Lent are obligatory days of abstinence.

To clarify, fasting is obligatory for any able-bodied Catholic age fourteen to fifty-nine. During a fast, a person is permitted to eat one full meal, as well as two smaller meals that together are not equal to a full meal. Fridays and other days of abstinence during Lent require Catholics to avoid the consumption of meat (though fish is allowed).

It's fairly simple, but (I write from experience) it's also easy to forget. In fact, it was only in my sixth year as a Catholic that I went a full Lent without accidentally eating meat on a Friday. This requirement may seem small, but it is amply demanding.

The Church urges us to observe these fasts and days of abstinence wholeheartedly by "offering up" our suffering (1 Pt 2:21). What this means is remembering that in giving up pleasures of the flesh, we unite ourselves to Christ; we become personal offerings united to his on the cross (Gal 2:20). In moments of difficulty, we can also remember the saints mentioned above as champions of mortifications. They rejoiced in any and all suffering (see 1 Pt 4:12–19).

Mortification is the best defense against sin, and it is also an important way we can make atonement for sins we have committed. Most importantly, mortification allows us to unite ourselves to Christ's sacrifice on the cross, to suffer with him, and to ask for graces for ourselves and for others.

Remember, while we must practice penance and mortification, we should always do so under the guidance of a trusted spiritual director. More than anything, submit to the penances the Church gives us and accept the crosses the Lord permits in your daily life. Zeal should drive us to do what God is genuinely asking us to do, no more and no less. Give mortifications their proper place in your spiritual exercises and you'll be amazed at the results.

38

Learn more about discernment and your vocation

When the Easter Vigil is over and you're fully received into the Church, you'll soon wonder, *"What's next?"* Let me assure you that you are asking the right question! The journey of Catholicism is lifelong, and it will require your attention, consideration, and patience. So let's explore how to understand your spiritual strengths and your vocation.

When I converted to Catholicism, I was in the middle of a master's degree program in business administration. I was also about a year into a great new career after exiting the military, and my wife was pregnant with our first child. Yet I felt a deep longing to study theology and work in the apostolate. I had huge dreams of working for big Catholic organizations, or even becoming a theology professor for a well-honored Catholic school. For a while, I even thought of getting a master's degree in theology, rather than business administration.

As I thought and prayed about it, however, I realized a vital life lesson. There was a ring on my finger and a mortgage bill on my desk. My priorities were clear. Ultimately, it was more important to continue the work that aided my vocation as a husband than it was to study theology as a hobby. The point is that subtle temptations, even in works of good intention, can cause us to misunderstand what God wants of us.

That was just my story. Yours may be entirely different, but you're probably still wondering "what's next?" Begin by understanding these two concepts: vocations and discernment.

Catholics use the term "vocation" to indicate what God has called us to in service of the Church. What God has called each of us to is the same: holiness. The Dogmatic Constitution on the Church, *Lumen Gentium*, assures us: "Therefore in the Church, everyone whether belonging to the hierarchy, or being cared for by it, is called to holiness, according to the saying of the Apostle: 'For this is the will of God, your sanctification.'"[11]

There are countless ways God provides for us to be sanctified because there are many different vocations. But the broad concept of a vocation is broken into two vocational categories: the primary vocation, where we ask, "What state of life has God called me to?" This could be the priesthood, religious life, married life, or the single life. Think to yourself, "Where am I right now?" Those primary vocation answers become more particular upon examination, which leads us to the other vocation: the particular vocation. For this, we ask, "What is God asking me to do within this vocation?" This might be the person we marry, the religious order we join, a parish priest or a monk, motherhood and fatherhood, and so on.

Answering these questions — especially the particular vocation — requires discernment. God doesn't only know us and see us perfectly, but he cares about every aspect of our life. Our God also gives us free will and reason to arrive at our decisions, and to act on them. Therefore, in discernment, our decisions should be based on a response to God's knowledge and love, and our desire to know and love him in return.

You're getting close to discerning what God has planned for your life. But you can't do it alone: you need help. That's why it's good to be Catholic: Let the Church assist you.

First, frequent the lives of the saints to see examples of the activity of discernment. Aloysius Gonzaga talked often with religious through his entire youth in order to be sure that the seminary was right for him. Discernment doesn't only apply to those considering a priestly vocation. Way before he founded the Society of Jesus, Ignatius of Loyola, obedient to his local superiors, sought a formal education prior to preaching in the streets. He knew he wanted to preach and yet allowed the wisdom of the Church to guide him.

Understanding what the Church teaches about various states of life also enables us to understand the vocational considerations. For example, the Church teaches that married couples must be open to life — important information for those who have never even considered parenthood. As a young man, Francis de Sales had always had a small desire to be a priest, but he did not force the issue. Instead, he followed his father's wishes and studied law. Upon returning home, he judged his unwillingness to marry as the suitable time to seriously consider the consecrated life.

If you're serious about a vocational decision, consider a spiritual director. Some confuse a spiritual director with a life coach, a prayer partner, or a counselor. But the purpose of a spiritual director is to help you listen more closely to discern the promptings of the Holy Spirit in your vocation. Spiritual direction will help you navigate, identify, and confirm significant life and vocational decisions. You might seek a spiritual director if you're discerning marriage, a religious life, the diaconate, or even changing careers or joining the apostolate.

It's not to say that "there are no wrong decisions," but however you move forward with your vocation, just make sure that you move forward while acknowledging God (Pr 3:6). Better to move intentionally to the source of life, than to rest content in the indecision of "whatever."

39

Holy water — keep it close and use it often

I used to think holy water was incredibly superstitious. "It's water! How silly and wasteful can Catholics be to dip their dirty hands in the same little container over and over and call it holy!" When left to our own wisdom, we often miss the perfect wisdom of the Faith present in Scripture and history. And the use of holy water goes back to time immemorial.

By now you have probably become used to seeing people walk into the church, dip their hands in the holy water font, and make the Sign of the Cross. Holy water is an important sacramental for Catholics, and a great source of graces and spiritual aid. It can be tempting to view it as mere superstition or empty ritual, but I assure you it is not. The use of holy water comes from the Old Testament and points to the reality of our baptism.

Water is the natural means of cleaning anything, and it is also the means by which God cleanses the earth and his people. When God created the earth, his Spirit moved over the waters, and then he spoke his Word (see Gn 1:1–2; Jn 1:1–5). This first creation foreshadows the new creation, as the *Catechism* echoes:

"Since the beginning of the world, water, so humble and wonderful a creature, has been the source of life and fruitfulness" (1218).

Water was God's choice when he cleansed the world of sin. This was prefigured in the story of Noah (Gn 6–7) and in the Israelites' crossing of the Red Sea when they escaped from Egypt (Ex 14). The Book of Leviticus prescribes various ritual purifications using water. These and several other Old Testament experiences with water prefigure our baptism in the New Covenant in Jesus Christ. The use of water was not diminished after its final revelation in the Sacrament of Baptism; rather, it was perfected and preserved for Christians.

The Church encourages us to use holy water. As a sacramental, its use can yield many blessings in our lives, including the following:

- **It helps us to overcome temptations.** The rite of providing holy water includes an exorcism prayer: "May all evil fancies of the foul fiend, his malice and cunning, be driven afar from the place where you are sprinkled. And let every unclean spirit be repulsed by Him who is coming to judge both the living and the dead and the world by fire."

- **It drives away sickness and future illnesses.** Holy water can help keep away illnesses of the body, mind, or soul. One of the prayers asks that the water would become "a medicine for body and soul for all who make use of you."

- **It removes venial sins.** Saint Thomas Aquinas wrote, "By the sprinkling of Holy Water the debt of venial sin is wiped out; but not always,

however, are all temporal punishments relin-
quished."[12]

- **It drives away the devil.** Saint Teresa of Ávila
  once said, "I often experience that there is nothing the devils flee from more, without returning, than holy water."[13]

I strongly encourage you to make use of holy water, not only
when you are in a church, but in your home as well. Your nearest
Catholic store should sell holy water vials and fonts, which you
can keep in your home. Your parish will have holy water available to you, so you can keep your vial full. Take advantage of
it! I have a colleague who keeps a small glass bottle of it on her
desk. My wife has a nice keychain that opens up to a tiny bottle
with a short squirt worth of holy water. At home, we keep a large
container. Whatever you choose, keep holy water close to you
and use it often.

When you're feeling tempted, ill, or spiritually dry, bless
yourself with holy water to combat the tricks of the devil. Holy
water can also be used to bless rooms and houses. Remember,
this is not superstitious. God chooses to use the simple things of
the world for his purposes, and holy water is his unique gift to
fight the spiritually unclean with the spiritually clean.

40

Have your house blessed

Home is where we gather to break bread with family and friends, and it's where we work, study, play, relax, and celebrate. We spend a good portion of our lives at home, whether we're sleeping, doing chores, eating, or watching Sunday football. Here we bring home our first child, we grieve loved ones we've lost, we discuss our life decisions, and we watch our kids grow. The home is a very special place. Whether you own or rent, live in an apartment or a townhouse, live alone or with a spouse and children, take the time to have your living space blessed by a priest.

You may have your house liturgically blessed at any time. In one case, I had to wait some time for an opening in my priest's schedule, but it is best to have a house blessed when you move in, if possible.

Go about it by casually asking your priest for the blessing. In some cases, you'll have to get with a secretary who helps manage the priest's schedule; but lock in that time. On the day of the blessing, I suggest opening your house to the priest as an honored guest: tidy up your home, have something prepared to eat and drink, and take a few moments to tell about your family and your history in the house (if you know about it). In one house we lived in, I knew the older couple before were militant atheists. That didn't change the blessing liturgy, but it did help bring everyone's awareness to the importance of driving out evil from the household.

If you have kids, this is a really cool moment for them. The priests who have blessed my house allow the kids to show the priest around the house, pointing to everything that needs a sprinkle (or a douse) of holy water. It becomes a fun event and a good learning opportunity.

Another long-standing Catholic tradition is to have it blessed around the feast of the Epiphany, known as "chalking the door." This doesn't require a liturgy, and you can even perform this blessing yourself. Some priests hand out blessed chalk on Epiphany for families to take home and mark their doorways with C+M+B for *Christus Mansionem Benedicat*: "May Christ bless this house." Then add the year. For example, a blessing on Epiphany 2020 looks like this: 20+C+M+B+20.

Having your home blessed secures it as a foothold of God's presence and that of his angels. It also cleanses the home of any spiritual evils that might be clinging to it because of things that occurred there in the past. Let the word of God, the authority of the priest, and the power of holy water clean and protect your home.

41

Grow in appreciation for sacred art

The term "sacred art" encompasses any work of art that pertains to things divine and is used in a public or private context for evangelization, contemplation, or education in the Faith. Sacred art is an enduring part of our faith, and it is important for any Christian — not just those with art and art history degrees. The Church has always shared the truths of revelation by expressing them in the arts.

There are two ways you can appreciate and promote sacred art. The first is by applying the principle of beauty to your daily life. You might not think of yourself as an artist, but you are. You might not think of your career, that blog you keep as a hobby, or your guitar chops as a means of expressing the sacred, but they are. Gardening, coaching, parenting, and acting are also excellent examples. These actions, and others like them, are your creations, your potential to express God's beauty and perfection. When we are inspired by our faith to commit ourselves to perfection, we can truly glorify God with whatever art we have the gifts to create.

The second way is by participating in or supporting serious and intentional training in the arts. You probably have a hobby. Maybe it's photography, graphic art, music, writing, or something similar. The arts are a special means of expressing the intellectual and spiritual beauty of God and truth, beauty and perfection. Allow your faith to mold your evaluation of the quality within the art, and let your faith inspire what you produce along with the level of skill applied to your given craft. In a word, seek perfection in art. In this way, you can participate in creation in a mysterious way. With this effort, you may turn many hearts and minds to the One who is beauty itself: Christ Jesus.

The next time you see a crucifix or a religious painting, take a moment to appreciate its uniqueness, its beauty, and the sense of workmanship that was poured into it. Likewise, the next time you are at a Catholic bookstore and think the art is overpriced, consider for a moment what price you would put on the proper expression of beauty and perfection, God and truth.

42

Get a spiritual director

We're not alone on the journey to heaven. There are many people on our team who keep us in line, strengthen us, and coach us. Our team includes our guardian angels and the saints, of course, as well as people who are still on this journey through life with us. We all need our whole team in order to get to where we are going. There is one key player many Catholics don't have, yet probably should: a spiritual director.

A spiritual director is not a counselor, a life coach, a confessor, a prayer partner, or a significant other. The spiritual director is the person who helps you listen closely to the Holy Spirit in discerning the promptings of God in your life. Spiritual direction is important for laypeople, whether they're discerning a vocation to the married life, priesthood, or religious life, or making their way through these vocations.

You might be wondering, "I pray, I go to Mass; why do I need a spiritual director?" The spiritual director is vital because there is one Holy Spirit. It is very easy to get into a rut when we attempt to navigate our spiritual life and vocation as a lone wolf. We truly need others to help us listen to what the Holy Spirit is directing us to do, both in the daily practice of our faith and in moments of big decision-making.

If you want to make your whole life about Jesus and you are honestly seeking to serve God, you need to find a spiritual director to help you. How do you go about finding a spiritual director? This can be very different depending on your unique needs and circumstances, but here are some general principles to guide your search:

- A good spiritual director will have a solid understanding of you as a person. This does not mean they know you intimately. In fact, they might not know you very well at all. But they should have a clear grasp of your needs and be able to communicate well with you. Remember: You're not looking for someone who tells you what you want to hear, but what you need to hear.

- Select someone you respect. You need someone you can look up to — not necessarily someone you want to be like, but whom you hold in high esteem. We learn best from our heroes, so make sure you choose someone whose faith you admire.

- Aim for wisdom as well as training. Many priests and others receive real training for the purpose of providing spiritual direction to others. Ensure your spiritual director has the training and experience to carry out this most important task. You can't afford to have someone "winging it" with your spiritual life.

- Make sure your spiritual director understands

your vocation. You don't want advice from someone who does not have a proper grasp on your given or prospective vocation. That said, you don't have to be pursuing the priesthood or religious life to get direction from a priest or religious.

- Last, your prospective spiritual director should have received his or her own direction. The last thing you want is someone who is just giving you advice off the cuff. If they are humble enough to receive direction and allow it to change them, they are much more likely to be able to give sound guidance.

Your most important decisions in life shouldn't be tackled alone. There are people in our Church who specialize in the guidance of souls, but it's up to you to seek them out. Pray for guidance as you search and trust that the Holy Spirit will lead you to the right person.

Even if you cannot find a dedicated spiritual director, direction in some form is always available. If your specific circumstances prevent you from meeting in person with a spiritual director, you might seek out a director who can correspond with you by phone, email, or letter. If nothing else, you can seek guidance from the writings of the saints, like Saints Francis de Sales or Josemaría Escrivá, who wrote many letters of spiritual direction in their lifetimes. In fact, most of the "spiritual classics" are simply collections of the letters exchanged between director and directee. If all else fails, the writings on the lives of our favorite saints often contain vital information for everyday life and important vocational decisions. By peering into their lives and decision-making processes, we gain invaluable wisdom and help.

43

Go on a retreat

A retreat is a multiday reclusion, passed usually in solitude and silence, giving particular emphasis to prayer and sometimes also penance. The concept of the retreat is deeply rooted in Christian history, notably sparked by Jesus spending forty days in the desert. With the advent of eremites (also known as hermits), and the rise of community life in monasteries, the spiritual advantages of withdrawing from the world became more evident. Through the centuries, religious congregations and clergy have instituted regulations for a frequency of retreats to maintain spiritual fitness. In modern times, all of the faithful are catching on to the idea of taking a retreat.

It's not hard to envision the practical needs for a retreat. Have you ever needed to "get away," not on vacation, but just to be by yourself and collect your thoughts for a time without the noise of the world and the anxiety of checking social media every few minutes? Men and women of all kinds need this respite, and Catholics have perfected the spiritual retreat. Your particular state of life doesn't have to accommodate a long-term hiatus from common life. A short-term retreat is often the catalyst for rapid spiritual growth and recovery.

The first kind of retreat I will recommend is a "do it yourself" (DIY) retreat. You make the plans, you set the tone, the intention, and the agenda. Here are my general steps to a quality DIY retreat:

- Set the intention. What do you hope to accomplish? What is the reason for the retreat? Is there a theme? Think about whether you need to make a decision, just have time to reflect, or require inspiration to get back into a spiritual routine.

- Find a setting far enough from home to be comfortable without requiring exhausting travel. Aim for a place that is silent and moderately secluded. If you can get into a seminary, a parish rectory, a monastery, or a priory, that's the perfect setting: chapels, daily Mass, and a place already inspiring to the Christian life is ideal.

- Set the agenda. Don't just show up and wing it. Make time for prayer, be sure you know when Mass and confession are available, schedule your meals, and be sure not to cram in too much — remember, this is a retreat, not a charge!

- Now, complete the retreat. Be prepared for unexpected changes and unforeseen inconveniences. Allow yourself to be open to the possibility that God is directing the show and giving you exactly the kind of retreat you need, even if it's not the one you had in mind.

- Finally, be considerate of your reintegration into regular life. Your family did not stop being a little dysfunctional, job stress did not disappear, and you shouldn't expect to return with the wisdom of Solomon. So, take care to be understanding of the chaos you might return to and aware of the humility and virtue you've been cultivating. By all means, use this as a motivation to plan your next retreat.

DIY retreats are fun and imaginative, but sometimes you don't want to do the planning, or you prefer the expertise of a seasoned retreat coordinator. Dotting the Catholic landscape are numerous retreat centers. These skillfully run venues have an abundance of services to offer to individuals, groups, and couples. Facilities often include chapels, prayer gardens, and a schedule to participate in the sacraments and adoration. Leave the challenge of planning your retreat to them, and allow them to provide spiritual guidance if you wish. If you're unsure how to find one, make a call to your diocese or ask your priest. They'll know!

Whatever you choose, make sure to maintain awareness for the seasons in life when a retreat is necessary. Catholic retreats offer a unique opportunity for soul-searching, decision-making, and true rejuvenation of body and soul.

44

Stay at a monastery or rectory

Many monasteries and seminary rectories open their doors to guests for retreats and meetings, and to travelers. It comes as a surprise to many that they're even available for use. I encourage you to look into it, as it's a great way to grow in your faith. The benefits are not to be overlooked, either.

The first time I stayed in a rectory, I was a little nervous. A friend recommended that I reserve a room at Kenrick-Glennon Seminary when traveling to St. Louis for a conference hosted by EWTN. I trusted him, but I also felt like I was taking advantage of the place. It was much cheaper than a hotel, and I'll say the service was much better, too. I kept asking myself why a seminary would host me, clean up after me, and so on. In spite of my discomfort, I went, and it was a fabulous experience. The room was small but cared for. It included a crucifix and a breviary, and it was quiet. I appreciated the sacred art on the walls, the seminary's library, twenty-four-hour chapel, and daily Mass, too.

I've continued to stay in seminaries and monasteries all over — from St. Louis to Kansas City, to Huntington on Long Island, locations in the deep South and the Northwest, and all across Europe. Recently, I had the pleasure of staying at a monastery on beautiful Lake Garda in the province of Brescia of northern Italy. It is run by the Sisters of Saint Elizabeth of Hungary. One of the sisters spoke fluent English and talked with me over a meal. She explained that having guests at the house served as a means of funding their missionaries in Brazil, Hungary, Russia, and in the Holy Land. She told me about the orphanages abroad, and how the sisters maintained the house while being responsible for taxes and local laws.

It was eye-opening. I realized how important it is that I continue to rely on these houses of prayer and religious life. As a layperson, whether I'm on vacation or a weeklong silent retreat, I'm directly funding missionaries who are giving children a home, teaching impoverished communities how to make clean water, and sharing the Gospel as Our Lord commanded. I was saving money and enjoying myself, but those were side benefits to supporting a mission much bigger than my weekend stay. The same goes for seminaries. Your stay might be brief, but you're ensuring young men are provided the education they need so they can live and serve as priests and religious, and so that those with more years under their belts can continue to mentor and impart wisdom to the next generation of priests.

Have no fear. Contact the local diocesan office when you're traveling to see where lodging and accommodations are available, or look for a nearby retreat house where you may receive some counsel and benediction from the resident religious.

45

Seek the grace to pray

Grace is a participation in the life of God (CCC 1997). In the Sacrament of Baptism, the Christian rises to new life, his soul made ready for participation in the Body of Christ and for involvement in the Church, where we are children of the Father.

The grace that fills the soul at baptism is called "sanctifying grace." Sanctifying grace is "a stable and supernatural disposition that perfects the soul itself to enable it to live with God, to act by his love" (CCC 2000). It is called a habitual grace, which is the permanent disposition to live and act in keeping with God's will. Once we have this grace, we can lose it only by mortal sin. We can grow in this grace through prayer and receiving the sacraments, and all Christians should pray continuously for an increase in sanctifying grace.

God also gives us particular graces to act according to his will, and these are called "actual graces." Actual graces help us perform good acts (as Jesus says, "for apart from me you can do nothing" [Jn 15:5]), sustain us in doing God's will, and help get us to confession when we have lost sanctifying grace through serious sin.

How do we grow in grace? Intimacy with God through

prayer and frequent reception of confession and the Holy Eucharist are the best means of obtaining graces. This works in a unique cycle: We pray for graces, yet we cannot pray for graces until we have the graces to pray. Knowing and loving God comes from prayer, and prayer emanates from a desire to love and know God — it's cyclical, and it always begins and ends with God's initiative, which is grace.

Our desire for prayer may diminish at times, and at other times may be robust and unstoppable. To avoid taking backward steps in the spiritual life, we need to pray for graces: We need to pray for the graces to pray, and even for the graces to pray for graces. We cannot live this supernatural life by our own efforts, because it is above our nature. This is why the instincts to pray must be developed through habitual prayer, always relying on God's grace.

Each time you pray, also pray for more graces to sustain your appetite for more prayer and to make you receptive to even more graces.

46

Indulge yourself,
categorically speaking

Indulgences are among the most misunderstood teachings of the Catholic Church. This misunderstanding has given rise to a lot of controversy, so it's important to have a good sense of what indulgences are.

According to the norms of the Church established by Pope Saint Paul VI in the Apostolic Constitution *Indulgentiarum Doctrina*, "an indulgence is the remission before God of the temporal punishment due sins already forgiven as far as their guilt is concerned, which the follower of Christ with the proper dispositions and under certain determined conditions acquires through the intervention of the Church which, as minister of the Redemption, authoritatively dispenses and applies the treasury of the satisfaction won by Christ and the saints."[14]

What does this mean? Well, when we sin, we need to make satisfaction. Although the guilt of our sin is removed in sacramental confession, the just punishment for sin still remains, which for most of us will happen in purgatory. This is where indulgences come in. An indulgence is the gift that frees us from the punishment due to our sin.

How do we gain indulgences? The Church has determined certain holy acts we can perform that can reduce or eliminate punishment in purgatory for sins that have already been forgiven of guilt. When identified by the Church, indulgences are attached to these acts. There are two kinds of indulgences: plenary and partial. A plenary indulgence remits all temporal punishment required to cleanse the soul from attachment to anything but God. A partial indulgence remits some of the temporal punishment due to sin.

As a prerequisite for obtaining an indulgence, a person must have a total detachment from sin, even venial. Then, to obtain a plenary indulgence, one must perform the particular indulgenced work, such as a pilgrimage or a specific devotion, with the specific intention of receiving the indulgence. Then there are three conditions that must be fulfilled: You need to go to confession (within several days), receive holy Communion, and pray for the intentions of the Holy Father. Even if you're not quite there yet, or you're not sure you are, seek out plenary indulgences anyway. You still receive a partial indulgence, and you grow in grace.

Here are just some of the many things you can do to gain indulgences (all taken from the *Enchiridion*, the authoritative guide for indulgences):

PLENARY

Note: You can receive only one plenary indulgence a day, whether for yourself or for the souls in purgatory.

- **Papal blessings**: You can gain a plenary indulgence when you "piously and devoutly" receive the blessing of the pope when imparted to Rome and the world (*Urbi et Orbi*). You can receive this blessing either in person or by radio, television, or Internet. This blessing is regularly given on Easter and Christmas, and occasionally at other times.

- **Cemetery visits**: A plenary indulgence is bestowed for visiting a cemetery and devoutly praying for the dead from November 1 to November 8 each year, when the Church remembers the dead in a special way.

- **Adoration of the cross**: You can gain a plenary indulgence during the Good Friday liturgy, if you devoutly adore the cross and kiss it.

- **A new priest's first Mass**: At the first Mass celebrated by a newly ordained priest, a plenary indulgence is granted to the priest and to the faithful who devoutly assist at the same Mass.

- **First holy Communion**: You probably already received this if you've had first Communion, but in addition to this, a plenary indulgence is granted to those who assist at the sacred ceremonies of someone else's first Communion.

- **The big four**: There are four things you can do just about any day that can gain a plenary indulgence: adoration of the Blessed Sacrament for at least a half-hour; pious reading of Sacred Scripture for at least a half-hour; praying the Stations of the Cross; and praying the Rosary in a church or with your family or a "pious association." Don't forget those four.

PARTIAL

- **Novena devotions**: A partial indulgence is provided to those who participate in a public novena before the feasts of Christmas, Pentecost, or the Immaculate Conception.

- **Recite the creeds**: Yup — getting a partial indulgence can be as easy as devoutly reciting either the Apostles' Creed or the Nicene Creed.

If you want to learn more, I suggest reading Pope Saint Paul VI's *Indulgentiarum Doctrina* and the *Enchiridion Indulgentiarum* (published in English as the *Manual of Indulgences*). In the first papal document, you will receive a solid foundation for understanding indulgences, and in the *Enchiridion* you'll have a desk reference for every type of ordinary approved indulgence, the norms, and the rules.

Now that you know about indulgences and how to obtain them, I urge you to make them a regular part of your life. One good way to get into this habit is to make the intention to gain indulgences in your morning prayer. Tell God that you want to obtain every indulgence you can that day.

47

Attend funerals and pray for the deceased

I was invited to a funeral once. It was for the wife of a man in our parish, but I had never met him or his deceased wife. What did I do? I went, and here's why: to pray for her soul and to provide spiritual comfort for those who survived her.

Today, a funeral is commonly believed to be the celebration of a person's life. While some parts of a funeral are rightly reserved to recognize the litany of accomplishments and excellent virtues of a person, that should not be the full focus of the ceremony. Instead, the Code of Canon Law states that Catholic funerals have three purposes: "In these funeral rites the Church prays for the spiritual support of the dead, it honors their bodies, and at the same time it brings to the living the comfort of hope" (1176.2).

The spiritual support we render at a funeral is pivotal for the deceased because, at the funeral Mass, we offer the Lord's sacrifice, the ultimate expiation for sins and provision for salvation. The Church recommends that there be a Mass offered for the repose of the soul of the deceased. The *Catechism of the Catholic*

Church states:

> In the Eucharist [offered for the repose of the
> soul of the deceased], the Church expresses her
> efficacious communion with the departed: of-
> fering to the Father in the Holy Spirit the sac-
> rifice of the death and resurrection of Christ,
> she asks to purify his child of his sins and their
> consequences, and to admit him to the Paschal
> fullness of the table of the kingdom.
>
> It is by the Eucharist thus celebrated that
> the community of the faithful, especially the
> family of the deceased, learn to live in commu-
> nion with the one who "has fallen asleep in the
> Lord," by communicating in the body of Christ
> of which he is a living member and, then, by
> praying for him and with him. (1689)

At a Christian funeral, we also honor the body of the deceased,
because the body of a baptized Christian is a dwelling place for
the Holy Spirit. Finally, funerals bring hope to the living. They
remind us of the fragility of life, the shortage of time we have on
earth, and the urgency to prepare ourselves for heaven.

So whether we know the person or not, and even if we didn't
necessarily like that person, it's a very good idea to go to their
funeral Mass, because we need to pray for their souls. We'll want
someone praying for our soul, too, right?

Catholic Life

48

Realize you're going to sin again and again

It's an unfortunate reality that we're human, and we make mistakes. And sometimes we make the same mistakes again and again. Being Catholic doesn't bring about instant holiness — we must work for the rest of our lives to overcome temptations, know Christ, and unite ourselves with him on the cross. We accept that we aren't perfect, but we serve a perfectly merciful God who perfectly offered himself as a perfect sacrifice for us, the imperfect, undeserving, repeat offenders.

Yes, we'll sin again. We cast stones at others. We fail to forgive. We fail to pray. We gossip. And so on and so forth. Satan then tells us that we've sinned too much, that there is no possible way that God can forgive us after what we've done, especially after we've said over and over that we'll quit. That, right there — if we cross through that door, we'll enter despair. Stepping through that door is deathly perilous for our souls. For in despair, we deny that God is who he is: good, holy, perfectly forgiving, perfectly loving, unchangeable. The truth (contrary to what the devil says) is that God is so immutable in his love for us that, no matter what, nothing can ever stop him from loving us, because that's who he is as God. And so, penitent children, we come back to him for the love that never fails.

It behooves us, then, to realize we'll sin. No, it is not okay to persist in sin. But we can and should recognize that we are always in constant need of God's graces to pull our lives together, and we need to rely on his never-failing mercy to be sustained and forgiven. You can count on this: God, as a loving Father, is always, always ready to forgive and strengthen us.

49

Invite your priest over for dinner

Invite your priest over for dinner. And don't make it a one-time thing. Invite him over regularly, if you both have time. Know a religious sister, too? Invite her over!

The biggest incentive for this is that it is a special opportunity to get to know your priest outside of normal church functions and liturgies. I've learned much about the priests we've had over for dinner: their hobbies, their thoughts on current events, the families they come from, and even a funny story or two they wouldn't share from the pulpit.

Another huge incentive, especially if you are a parent, is to encourage vocations. In my household, we make every opportunity to show our kids that being a priest or religious is a normal, enjoyable, and rewarding way of life. Our goal as parents is to be sure there is no stone unturned, so our kids regularly have the opportunity to pepper our priest and religious friends with questions about religious life and the discernment of their vocation.

Priests and religious are also very busy people. Offering

them a home-cooked meal and a few hours to relax and enjoy a relaxing conversation can also bless them in ways we might not fully appreciate — but I've never been turned down, even if it's a rain check, and that tells me they enjoy the experience, too.

When we invite our priest over for dinner, we accomplish several things. We open our households to invaluable discipleship opportunities. Our marriages are gifted with beautiful confirmations of our love and productivity. The priest is given a satisfying meal, and will likely offer a priestly blessing. And perhaps more important than all these, we can see one gracious benefit rise above the rest: the promotion of religious vocations. When we get to know our priest and other religious on a personal level, our children can witness the reality and down-to-earth nature of religious life. Trust me; your priest will not say no — but don't be offended if he has trouble finding an available night.

50

Become a part-time vegetarian

In most ancient cultures, meat was considered a delicacy, and the proverbial "fattened calf" was not slaughtered unless there was something to celebrate. As an act of penance, it was standard procedure to abstain from meat. All the Desert Fathers abstained from meats. Saint Charles Borromeo rarely ever ate meat. Young Saint Aloysius Gonzaga never consumed it, though he sat in the dining halls of King Philip II of Spain. Trappists, Cistercians, Benedictines, and Franciscans all have had a tradition of a vegetarian diet, to which many still adhere.

While the rules on fasting have recently changed (see section 37 on mortification, including fasting), the Church still recommends abstinence on all Fridays of the year, not just during Lent. In 1966, Pope Saint Paul VI published *Paenitemini*, an encyclical on fasting and abstinence. He clarifies: "In the first place, Holy Mother Church, although it has always observed in a special way abstinence from meat and fasting, nevertheless wants to indicate in the traditional triad of 'prayer — fasting — charity' the fundamental means of complying with the divine precepts of penitence" (chapter 3).

He continues: "The Church, while preserving — where it can be more readily observed — the custom (observed for many centuries with canonical norms) of practicing penitence also through abstinence from meat and fasting, intends to ratify with its prescriptions other forms of penitence as well, provided that it seems opportune to episcopal conferences to replace the observance of fast and abstinence with exercises of prayer and works of charity."

Though the rules, strictly, have altered, many devoted Catholics still make efforts to avoid meat, particularly on Fridays throughout the year — not just during Lent. There are fantastic benefits. Since Fridays are a day of penance, giving up meat on Friday recognizes the death of Christ and is also a mortification of the flesh. Giving up something that's, in essence, a luxury is meritorious for our self-control and for our souls.

Just in case you are having doubts and thinking you'd never be able to give up your wings and beer night, give it a while to sink in and pray about becoming a part-time vegetarian — it's only once a week!

As a final note, the USCCB governs the disciplines of fasting and abstinence required for Lent. In summary, Ash Wednesday and Good Friday are obligatory days of fasting and abstinence for Catholics, and Fridays during Lent are obligatory days of abstinence. This applies to Catholics ages fourteen and up.

51
Have a beer

Before water-purification systems, fermented beverages were the preferred choice of most civilizations. Wine, distilled spirits, and other brews were typical, but before each of these came beer.

From China to Bavaria, beer could be made with several kinds of grain using several techniques. Baking, mixing, aging, and experimenting led to a variety of brews for trade and for personal enjoyment. And when the great plagues of Europe broke out, because clean water was difficult to procure but brewing could be done for cheap, several great brands were born: Stella Artois in Belgium, La Trappe in the Netherlands, and Smithwicks in Scotland.

During this time, numerous religious orders and monasteries began to craft beer to help those in need, and monks continued this tradition of excellence, pursuing perfection in brewing to honor God with their craft and their prayer. To this day, Trappist, Benedictine, and Carmelite abbeys still make some of the most enjoyable and celebrated beers in the world.

Celebrate your faith and honor the devotion of the priests and religious who pour their love of the Father into every drop they produce. The Catholic life sometimes means being serious about relaxation and enjoying a taste of perfection. Anything that reflects perfection reflects the nature of God, which is the primary reason why so many monks dedicate themselves to this craft.

The patron saint of brewers, Saint Arnold of Metz, said, "From man's sweat and God's love, beer came into the world." Go to your nearest beer store and look for brews such as Chimay, Westmalle, Rochefort, and (my personal favorite) Tripel Karmeliet. Then go home and read some Dante, Augustine, or Aquinas. Pop a top, watch the bubbles build, and enjoy a friendly dialogue with your Catholic friends or read a good book. Beer, scholarly dialogue, and reading — when well-tempered — go well together. Which is why the virtuous Saint Brigid of Ireland is quoted to have said: "I would like a great lake of beer for the King of Kings and I would like to be watching heaven's family drinking it through all eternity."

52

Don't be superstitious

We Catholics do some admittedly weird things, but it's not because we are superstitious. It is important to understand the difference between devotional practices and superstitions, because on the surface they can look similar.

Consider this example: Your Catholic neighbor puts up a "For Sale" sign in their front yard, and they also bury a Saint Joseph statue. When you ask them why, they explain that it is good luck and that it might help sell the house.

This is a problem. Catholics do not do anything for luck. Do you recall how Matthias was chosen to be the successor of Judas (the disciple who betrayed Jesus)? The apostles "cast lots," meaning they rolled the dice. But they did not cast lots for good luck — instead they prayed, and they trusted that the outcome would show them God's will (Acts 1:21–26).

In the example above, the Catholic neighbor, lacking a more complete understanding of his faith, misrepresents a common Catholic practice. Praying to the saints for help is good and necessary, but superstition is a sin, so as Catholics, we need to avoid it. Here is what the *Catechism* has to say:

The first commandment forbids honoring gods other than the one Lord who has revealed himself to his people. It proscribes superstition and irreligion. Superstition in some sense represents a perverse excess of religion; irreligion is the vice contrary by defect to the virtue of religion.

Superstition is the deviation of religious feeling and of the practices this feeling imposes. It can even affect the worship we offer the true God, e.g., when one attributes an importance in some way magical to certain practices otherwise lawful or necessary. To attribute the efficacy of prayers or of sacramental signs to their mere external performance, apart from the interior dispositions that they demand, is to fall into superstition. (2110–2111)

Continuing our example of the Saint Joseph statue, we cross over the line into superstition if we believe that an object in itself aids the efficacy of our prayers. Prayers are dependent upon faith and upon providence, not luck. Holy images assist and increase our faith, and inasmuch as a Saint Joseph statue increases our confidence in prayer, it is a good practice to keep it visible as we pray for the house to sell. But burying the statue is not advisable. It's proper to bury a statue only when it is broken or otherwise needs to be disposed of.

This example is a prevalent one, but the principles may be applied to a spectrum of common practices, like keeping a statue of Saint Anthony on your dashboard to make sure you don't get lost, or hanging a Rosary from your rearview mirror to avoid an accident. Instead, keep these things there to remind you to pray.

Superstition is the fruit of fear. Catholics, like everyone else, experience anxiety and desperation, wanting to do just about anything to get the outcomes they feel they need. But God already knows what you need, and he loves you. That's more comforting than any superstition.

When you pray, and especially when you use sacramentals, do it with a genuine interior spirit of prayer and confidence in God's providence. His primary interest is bringing us to his mansion with many rooms, which is our eternal home.

53

Discover other ways to live your faith

There are numerous Catholic traditions to discuss and try out, but I cannot mention them all. Christians in the earliest days of the Church developed secret signals, drew crosses in the dirt, and carved crosses into seemingly everything they could touch. Some traditions have come and gone; they belonged to particular times, circumstances, or cultures. Others have endured throughout the life of the Church. I'll list some of my favorites here, and you can try them out if they grab your interest. If you want to learn about others, I highly recommend *Catholic Traditions and Treasures* by Helen Hoffner or *Around the Year with the Von Trapp Family* by Maria Von Trapp.

A SAINTLY GARDEN

The Bible contains several references to flora as symbols of holiness and divinity. The prophet Isaiah compares flowers to God's faithful (Is 40:6), and Jesus uses blossoms and fruit as signs for faith and obedience (see Mk 11:12–25). Take a look at a few images of the saints, and you'll notice many of them involve some sort of flower — often a white lily, representing virginal purity. Even some flowers themselves are named after saints; rosemary and marigold, for instance, honor the Blessed Mother.

Romans or others who could afford it kept the central parts of their houses as gardens, and those who were Christians kept this as a special place of dedication to the beauty of the Lord. Christians, instead of including marble statues of pagan mythological figures, added statues of the saints to their gardens. This tradition continues today.

If you have a garden, go ahead and add a statue to it — Mary, Saint Joseph, and Saint Francis are popular choices. Stone naturally enhances the beauty of flowers, and images of the saints remind us of their holiness and God's presence. When choosing flowers, here are a few you might want to select for what they represent: violets (modesty and piety); columbines (the path of the holy); snowdrops and white lilies (purity); juniper (refuge and safety — calling to mind the Holy Family's flight to Egypt); marigolds (riches of faith); and lily of the valley and iris (tears and sorrow). Of course, the rose is the queen of all flowers — and who do we honor as queen of heaven and earth? The Blessed Mother, of course!

KISSING A BISHOP'S RING

Rings can be symbols of spiritual realities. Wedding rings represent the wholeness, beauty, and indissoluble nature of marriage. Rings in the ancient world were gifts for athletic and military accomplishments. And traditionally, rings represent the power of princes and kings. Because hands are among the most noticeable appendages, it is natural that status, achievement, and power were worn on the finger. Therefore, it was customary to kiss the ring of those who were advanced in rank or class. The same became a tradition of Catholics, and it has been a long-standing custom to kiss the ring of a bishop. In this, you aren't personally reverencing an individual bishop, but rather symbolically showing your respect and fidelity to the apostles. The apostles were the princes of the Church; modern bishops, through episcopal succession, represent and take on this apostolic authority. When we kiss the ring of a bishop, we perform an act of humility to the institution of the Church, Christ's bride, that is vested in the holiness and divinity of Jesus himself.

SAINT JOSEPH'S ALTAR

A favorite tradition of Catholics — especially in New Orleans, but anywhere with a Sicilian or Italian heritage — is the Saint Joseph Altar. The heart of the tradition says that in the Middle Ages, in Sicily, there was a terrible drought, which caused a nationwide famine. Catholics began to pray for the intercession of San Giuseppe (Saint Joseph). When the rains came and the crops returned, the farmers showed their gratitude for his beneficence by offering the fruits of their labors to their less fortunate neighbors.

There can be variation among communities, but the altar is often shaped like a cross, with three levels, one for each Person of the Trinity. On the uppermost level, in the center position, there is usually a good-sized statue of Saint Joseph. Each level is typically draped in white cloth and decorated with beautiful and symbolic objects, including flowers, fruits, holy icons and images, crucifixes, and candles. The size is up to the person or group making the altar.

The food on the altar is particular but also leaves room for creativity. There must be no meat — after all, Saint Joseph's feast day is on March 19, usually occurring during Lent, which historically was completely meatless. There is fish as well as other local seafood. Wines, pasta dishes, meatless tomato sauce, cakes, and bread are also common. The point is to fill up every available square inch on the table with food! It sounds scrumptious, so who is invited? Visitors are allowed to partake at some altars, but traditionally, all the food is given to the poor or sent to orphanages or homes for the elderly.

54

Read the documents of the Second Vatican Council

Imagine that before you got married, your spouse had written a short book. In that book, she wrote her expectations about herself, and her expectations of you. She also wrote on the most pertinent ideas about what she believes, and what she plans for you both to do, together, to achieve a successful marriage. You'd be crazy not to read that book, wouldn't you?

Well, the Church, the Bride of Christ, has continually addressed the issues she is facing in every age through ecumenical councils. And fortunately for us, the documents of the most recent council (the Second Vatican Council, also known as Vatican II) are easily available for our learning and guidance. In these documents, the Church outlines her expectations of herself and of each of her members (including you). She explains what we believe about the most pertinent issues facing the modern age, and she discusses her hopes for how the clergy, religious, and laity may achieve success together.

Catholics who have the time and ability should read the documents of Vatican II. While you go to Mass, tithe your hard-earned money to the Church, and ask God to tell you what to do with your life, take the time to read the documents that chart the course of the Church for the next several generations. In addition to knowing where the Church sees herself in the modern world, it benefits every Catholic to wonder, "How did we get here?," and find out.

By reading the documents of Vatican II, you'll gain valuable knowledge in apologetics, evangelization, Church history, and theology. More accurately, you'll understand what the Church thinks is the vocational purpose and direction of the family, religious, and the laity. You'll also get a fair amount of instruction on the Church's position on critical modern issues like arms, war, education, politics, and more.

Here's a short synopsis of the three important documents I encourage you to begin with:

- *Dei Verbum*: The purpose of the Dogmatic Constitution on Divine Revelation is to "set forth authentic doctrine on divine revelation and how it is handed on, so that by hearing the message of salvation the whole world may believe, by believing it may hope, and by hoping it may love" (*DV* 1).

- *Lumen Gentium*: The Dogmatic Constitution on the Church is precisely what it sounds like. The Council Fathers "[desire] now to unfold more fully to the faithful of the Church and to the whole world its own inner nature and universal mission" (*LG* 1). The document thoroughly covers the purpose, identity, and mission of the Church, from the people of God in general, to the hierarchy, to the laity.

- ***Gaudium et Spes***: This document is the Pastoral Constitution on the Church in the Modern World, and it is a treasury of information on everything from politics, to war, to social justice, to the dignity of the human person. It is a critical document in our times, where the Church's views are very unpopular.

55

Find your people

Becoming a Catholic — heck, even *being* a Catholic — often requires a particular set of social skills. Catholics have to be thick-skinned while continually seeking the good of others. And sometimes it might feel like there are absolutely no Catholics within reach for friendship and fellowship. But in the twenty-first century, that's a stretch. You pretty much have to live under a rock to not get into a social scene. And I'm not just referring to Facebook groups and Twitter circles. You may be surprised to find a dedicated and thriving Catholic group right under your nose, just waiting for you to join them. Maybe that group is in person, or maybe it's online, but chances are good there's a group for everyone. It's up to you to go out there and find your people. And if you do not see what you want, why not make that group yourself?

I'm involved a little everywhere. In my parish, I helped start a Wednesday night men's burger-and-beer group. Twice a month we find a new place in the area (or at our homes), and we have a short message, pray, and break bread — two pieces of a bun, to be exact — together. I also do my best to maintain relationships online. I'm active on social media, and I've also found people in the online gaming world who are Catholic; we have short get-togethers while playing our favorite video games. These groups have become some of the most productive conversations and friendships I've had for the benefit of my soul.

You can find yours, too. If you're not sure where to start, I suggest you look first at your parish bulletin or website, where you'll likely find a list of groups or ministries. You can also look online for like-minded Catholics. Twitter, Facebook, Reddit, and LinkedIn are great places to start. Your people are out there: campers, hikers, fishers, fashionistas, mothers, essential oil lovers, Tolkien fanatics, philosophers, perfectionists, and sinners. Find your people. "For where two or three are gathered in my name, there am I in the midst of them" (Mt 18:20).

Customs, Rules, and Basic Etiquette

56
Bishops, priests, and deacons

It's not the end of the world if you don't know how to address the pope — though let's hope you get the chance — but it's always handy to know who you're talking to and how to render them appropriate courtesies.

There are three divisions in the Sacrament of Holy Orders. The three divisions are deacon, priest, and bishop, and each is successively obtained before the other by ordination. Priests and bishops (presbyterate and episcopate, respectively) are the ministerial degrees of participation in the sacrament, and deacons are meant to serve these two. For more reading on deacons, priests, and bishops, read the *Catechism*, paragraphs 1536–1600.

- **Deacons**: All priests are first ordained as deacons. This happens, usually, one year before being ordained to the priesthood. It's called a transitional diaconate, which is a fancy way of saying that they're a deacon now but in the process of becoming a priest. Permanent deacons have been ordained as deacons, but will remain in that position of service either for their parish or the diocese. They may be married men, and are typically over thirty-five years old, depending on the rules of their episcopal see. Whether transitional or permanent, you can call a deacon "Deacon."

- **Priests**: You'll probably meet many priests in your life as a Catholic. A priest in the Catholic Church is a man who has been ordained to fulfill the duties of celebrating the Sacrifice of the Mass, hearing confession, giving absolution, and administering the other sacraments *in persona Christi* (meaning "in the person of Christ"). Priests also perform other duties of pastoral ministry and, sometimes, administration. Priests are called "Father," although if you are addressing a letter to them or referring to them in a formal way, you would call them Reverend [First Name Last Name]. There are a few different kinds of priests to know of:

A **diocesan priest** serves within his diocese, unless sent to some other service by his bishop, to whom he promises obedience.

A **religious priest** (like a Dominican) vows obedience to his superior, usually called a "provincial," and typically will live in community with one or more priests of his order.

A **monastic priest** vows obedience to his abbot

(if living in an abbey) or prior (in a priory). Depending on the specific order, ministry, or duties of "labor," some may often be found outside of the monastery. For example, some monks labor in the creation of beer away from their monastery, and others are assigned the duties of evangelizing abroad or teaching.

- **Bishops**: Bishops have the fullness of Holy Orders. A bishop is directly appointed by the pope to oversee a diocese. They are priests, and they are entrusted with the responsibility to ordain new priests and deacons — they are the only ones who are vested with this power. Some bishops are of higher rank than other bishops, and these are known as "archbishops." You should address all bishops and archbishops as "Your Excellency" and refer to them as "His Excellency."

- **Cardinals**: A cardinal is an elevated member of the clergy (though, historically, not always a priest!). The last "lay cardinal" was Teodolfo Mertel, who died in 1899. Since then, Pope Benedict XV revised sections of the Code of Canon Law to state that only priests or bishops may be chosen as cardinals. The pope makes cardinals. Their primary duty is to elect the bishop of Rome, but they are often summoned in groups or as individuals to whatever the pope needs, often in the form of synods or other meetings. Other cardinals hold power in the various offices of the curia and bear a high degree of responsibility of the ministry of souls. You should address all cardinals as "Your Eminence" and refer to them as "His Eminence."

- **Popes**: The pope, the Vicar of Christ, is Our Lord's representative on earth and the leader of the Church (see section 58 to learn how he is elected). He — since there is only one at a time — is the Supreme Pontiff, which means "greatest bridge-builder." The pope is the successor of Saint Peter, to whom the keys of the kingdom of heaven were given, and he is responsible for the entire flock of Christians. He also holds a civil position as the governmental head of Vatican City, the smallest country in the world. Should you have the opportunity to address the pope directly, you would call him "Your Holiness" and refer to him as "His Holiness."

As mentioned above, there is only ever one pope at a time. Many are confused by the situation in the Church as of this writing, in which we have one active and one retired pope. Does this mean we have two popes? The simple answer is no. In 2013, Pope Benedict XVI abdicated his position as Supreme Pontiff, and Pope Francis was elected. Once one pope stepped down and the other was elected, there was one single pope. Benedict, by his own choice, is no longer the pope. He requested to be called "Pope Emeritus," which is an honorific title that simply indicates he is the previous holder of that office. He later realized that this incited confusion and requested to simply be called Father Benedict. Unable to enforce this request, however, he stuck with the title Pope Emeritus Benedict XVI for the public at large. He continues to wear the white cassock of the pope because his status as a living successor of Saint Peter has not changed.

57

The role of the bishop

The role and position of a bishop is among the most honorable and essential in the Church. Bishops are more than merely the people in charge. They are indeed the princes of the Church and rightfully called our shepherds. As our shepherds, our bishops are owed a special reverence, as we acknowledge that they bear a tremendous responsibility.

One of the earliest bishops, Saint Ignatius of Antioch, wrote in a letter: "Wherefore it is fitting that ye also should run together in accordance with the will of the bishop who by God's appointment rules over you. ... Let us be careful, then, not to set ourselves in opposition to the bishop, in order that we may be subject to God. ... It is manifest, therefore, that we should look upon the bishop even as we would look upon the Lord himself, standing, as he does, before the Lord."[15]

The Fathers of Vatican II teach us:

> The bishops themselves, however, having been appointed by the Holy Spirit, are successors of the apostles as pastors of souls. Together with the supreme pontiff and under his authority

they are sent to continue throughout the ages the work of Christ, the eternal pastor. Christ gave the apostles and their successors the command and the power to teach all nations, to hallow men in the truth, and to feed them. Bishops, therefore, have been made true and authentic teachers of the faith, pontiffs, and pastors through the Holy Spirit, who has been given to them.[16]

The *Catechism* reminds the faithful: "Through the ordained ministry, especially that of bishops and priests, the presence of Christ as head of the Church is made visible in the midst of the community of believers. In the beautiful expression of Saint Ignatius of Antioch, the bishop is *typos tou Patros*: he is like the living image of God the Father" (1549).

As Pope Pius XII expressed it, "Though each bishop is the lawful pastor only of the portion of the flock entrusted to his care, as a legitimate successor of the apostles, he is, by divine institution and precept, responsible with the other bishops for the apostolic mission of the Church."[17]

These men are responsible for the souls of men, and they must take this responsibility seriously. The slightest of poor decisions, one careless mistake, or a minor act of destroying transparency and public trust can have ramifications for hundreds or thousands of souls. This is not because a bishop's sins are imparted on the faithful, but because he is their shepherd. His sins can cause his flock to sin, despair, and turn away from the Lord, perhaps forever. The bishop is truly a head of the Church, and when the head fails, the body hurts.

It's critical to understand how vital the bishops are, and the proper relationship we the faithful must have with their position. The key word here is "position." We revere the position, even if we don't necessarily like the person under the chasuble and robes. That being said, some bishops create situations in which absolute obedience from their flock is impossible. For example, the heretical bishops of history, such as Arius and Nestorius (whose famous heresies you can read about in section 87 of this book), cannot be true shepherds when their teachings no longer represent the truth. The same goes for the bishops who abuse their power, such as those who collected alms as wealth in the thirteenth through the sixteenth centuries, and those who in recent times have turned a blind eye to — and even abetted in — criminal behavior.

But as with any controversy, faith, goodwill, and the benefit of the doubt serve us in good stead. When information travels at lightspeed, and opinions spread like wildfire, your best bet is to be the stone at the bottom of the river: smooth, durable, and firmly planted with the wisdom of patience, not moved by every toss and turn of the flow. Remember Paul's words to the church in Corinth: "Therefore, my beloved brethren, be steadfast, immovable, always abounding in the work of the Lord, knowing that in the Lord your labor is not in vain" (1 Cor 15:58).

58

Papal elections and how they work

How a pope is elected is a fairly simple procedure nowadays: The entire College of Cardinals gathers to vote until a two-thirds majority decision is reached and the nominee accepts. This is called a conclave.

However, many make the assumption, which can frustrate the faith of the most reliable believer, that the Holy Spirit chooses the pope. Logic and faith inform us differently, though. We believe in free will, both in everyday decisions like what we eat and say, and in big decisions like career paths and vocations. We also believe in the wisdom and guidance provided by the Holy Spirit. Scripture tells us, "But when he, the Spirit of truth, comes, he will guide you into all the truth. He will not speak on his own; he will speak only what he hears, and he will tell you what is yet to come" (Jn 16:13).

The Bible also tells us that we may ask for wisdom, and God will grant it: "If any of you lacks wisdom, let him ask God, who gives to all men generously and without reproaching, and it will be given him" (Jas 1:5). The wisdom and guidance of the Holy

Spirit must coincide with free will. So when a man and a woman enter into a marriage, they enter into a sacred union as a matter of choice, but they can form this selection through prayer and careful discernment. The same happens when a pope is elected. Cardinals, men who have free will, gather with the intention of selecting a pontiff who will successfully lead the Church, while also praying that their nomination will be what God wills. They have free will to pray, listen, and act; and God promises guidance and wisdom.

Some ask a very reasonable and important question: Does the Holy Spirit choose the pope? When cardinals participate in a conclave, they have free will to choose who the next pope will be. It requires a lot of prayer, a lot of consideration, and frankly, a lot of listening to other cardinals and conversations outside the conclave. They do their best and there are wonderful moments when the decision is unanimous, but the Holy Spirit cannot intercede in place of free will. We need to understand this as well. Why? Two reasons: the bad popes, and buyer's remorse.

It's important to be aware that the Church has had some very bad popes. Pope John XII had a mistress and Pope Urban VI tortured cardinals. The point of all this: The successors of Peter have not all been saintly. It's vital to remember that God's providence allows for this to happen, but God does not choose for us to have bad popes.

The other reason to understand this lesson is that, sadly, some Catholics get a form of buyer's remorse. They are jubilant on the day a pope is elected and makes his beautiful opening sermon. Then, over the next weeks, the news networks report of the good works of his life and ministry. Confidence grows. But, over time, they hear about this rumor or that misquote, or this scandal and that accusation. And because the pope is such a critical component of our faith, when that foundation is shaken, they get a form of buyer's remorse. They lose confidence in a pope, and this can cause them to lose hope in the Church.

Keeping a level head about the humanity of a pope and his election will help you survive the moments of controversy, and it can also be a unique opportunity to grow in faith — because God chooses the weak to lead his people. The Bible tells us:

> But God chose the foolish things of the world to shame the wise; God chose the weak things of the world to shame the strong. God chose the lowly things of this world and the despised things — and the things that are not — to nullify the things that are, so that no one may boast before him. It is because of him that you are in Christ Jesus, who has become for us wisdom from God — that is, our righteousness, holiness and redemption. Therefore, as it is written: "Let the one who boasts boast in the Lord." (1 Cor 1:27–31)[18]

59

Get comfortable with nuns and monks

Understanding the various kinds of religious states and the terms associated will help any Catholic appreciate the variety our Church offers for those sensing the call to a unique state of life. Perhaps at some point, you too might sense a call to an appropriate state of life within the Church. Religious life, or the consecrated life, refers to living in a stable state of life recognized by the Church, in which a person dedicates their whole life to God in imitation of Christ through a particular public profession. Some religious also take specific vows, intrinsic to a state of life, usually according to a religious order's norms, which may include articles like poverty and obedience.

SISTERS AND NUNS

A Catholic nun is a woman who lives as a contemplative in a monastery, either cloistered or semicloistered. She professes perpetual solemn vows to live the evangelical counsels of poverty, chastity, and obedience. The ministry and prayer life of a nun is lived out in the monastery, but focused on the good of the whole world.

A religious sister, on the other hand, lives and prays in a convent but ministers in some active or apostolic work, such as the works of mercy, teaching, nursing, or many other ministries that take the Gospel to others, wherever they are. She professes perpetual simple vows of poverty, chastity, and obedience.

The terms "nun" and "sister" are frequently used interchangeably in common dialogue, but now you know the difference. Both nuns and sisters fall into the category of "women religious," and both are addressed as "Sister." The religious who is the head of a particular community is often called "Mother" and given the title of Mother Superior, Prioress, or Abbess.

BROTHERS

Some religious men who do not receive the Sacrament of Holy Orders live their lives with professions to poverty, chastity, and obedience. Many brothers live in a community that observes a particular rule of life, such as the Benedictines. Their charism is predicated on building the soul of their community through a common mission and communal prayer. We address these men as "Brother."

VOWS

As you might have noticed, different religious make different types of vows, solemn or simple. *The New Commentary on the Code of Canon Law* explains the distinction this way:

> The older religious orders (monastic, canon regulars, mendicants, Jesuits) have perpetual solemn vows, and the more recent apostolic congregations have perpetual simple vows. The chief difference between the two is that religious who profess a solemn vow of poverty renounce ownership of all their temporal goods, whereas religious who profess a simple vow of

poverty have a right to retain ownership of their patrimony (an estate, endowment or anything inherited from one's parents or ancestors) but must give up its use and any revenue.[19]

Upon making profession, many men and women religious select a new religious name. This practice is a long-standing tradition with biblical roots, and it symbolizes entering into a new state in life. How a religious receives their name differs from one religious community to the next: for some, the choice is autonomous, and for others, it is ultimately up to the superior. Addressing these religious, one would refer to them as Brother/Sister [New Name].

60

When to genuflect and when to bow

Catholics seem to do a lot of bowing and genuflecting, and it can be confusing and frustrating to try to learn when to do these things. Here are some basic guidelines.

BOWING

According to the General Instruction of the Roman Missal (commonly called the "GIRM"):

> A bow signifies reverence and honor shown to the persons themselves or to the signs that represent them. There are two kinds of bows: a bow of the head and a bow of the body.

> a)   A bow of the head is made when the three Divine Persons are named together and at the names of Jesus, of the Blessed Virgin Mary, and of the Saint in whose honor Mass is celebrated.

b) A bow of the body, that is to say a profound bow, is made to the altar; during the prayers *Munda cor meum* (Almighty God, cleanse my heart) and *In spiritu humilitatis* (Lord God, we ask you to receive); in the Creed at the words *Et incarnatus est* (by the power of the Holy Spirit … and became man); in the Roman Canon at the words *Supplices te rogamus* (Almighty God, we pray that your angel). The same kind of bow is made by the deacon when he asks for a blessing before the proclamation of the Gospel. Also, the priest bows slightly as he speaks the words of the Lord at the consecration.[20]

These are the instructions for Mass, but mostly for the priest. You'll want to concern yourself mainly with the place in the Nicene Creed where the congregation bows. In every Mass when we profess the Creed, we bow from the words "by the power of the Holy Spirit" to "and became man," reverencing the great gift of Christ's incarnation. And as the middle paragraph mentions, a slight inclination of the head is appropriate reverence when we hear or speak the name of Jesus, and the Trinity, at Mass or in other prayers and conversation.

GENUFLECTING

What does it mean to genuflect? The GIRM says: "A genuflection, made by bending the right knee to the ground, signifies adoration, and therefore it is reserved for the Most Blessed Sacrament, as well as for the Holy Cross from the solemn adoration during the liturgical celebration on Good Friday until the beginning of the Easter Vigil."[21]

The GIRM adds that "all who pass before the Most Blessed

Sacrament genuflect, unless they are moving in procession." A different resource, called the Ceremonial of Bishops, mentions in several areas to give a deep bow to the altar, the table of sacrifice.[22] In the case where there is a tabernacle with the Blessed Sacrament present on the altar (or perhaps behind the altar), the former takes precedence: genuflect to the Eucharist.

Things like genuflections and bowing might seem like "the small stuff," but these outward gestures are expressions of what we believe: Christ became man to save us, and he remains with us, truly present in the Blessed Sacrament. He is there, and the reverence and obedience we give to our God should be evidenced in how we behave.

61

Names of objects
used in Mass

It's likely that at some point while attending Mass, you have wondered why something belongs in a particular spot, why some things have to be carried, held, or read by a specific person, or what this or that thingamajig is called. Don't worry — this is normal, and the Mass can take a couple of years to understand and appreciate fully. Even many lifelong Catholics don't know what everything is called!

Personally, I always receive holy Communion on the tongue. One morning as I went up to receive, sticking my tongue out as I always do, the administer of holy Communion fumbled the Host — it did not stick to my tongue but to his finger, and the Host dropped to the floor. Speaking of it later, I described it like this: "The little plate thingie didn't catch the Host."

It's not the end of the world if I don't know that "the little plate thingie" is called a paten. But proper appreciation begets faith, and faith desires more appreciation. So I want to help you by going over the instruments and vessels you'll see in almost every Mass — you might need to recall the names of them at some point, but more importantly, knowing them can help you grow in appreciation for the Mass.

INSTRUMENTS AND VESSELS

- **Chalice** (CHAL-is): The large cup that the priest uses to consecrate the wine to become the Blood of Christ. These vary in style and shape, but it's required that the inner portion that holds the Precious Blood be at least covered with precious metal — gold or silver. With special exception, the General Instruction of the Roman Missal allows for precious woods, metals, and other materials that do not absorb liquids, which is why you might see olive wood chalices from the Holy Land, or fine ceramic ones from Italy (328–330).

- **Communion Cup**: The cup in which the congregation receives the Precious Blood. These are kept, along with many of the other Mass essentials, at what is known as the "credence table."

- **Ciborium** (si-BO-ree-um): "Cibo" is the Latin word for "food," so it is fitting that as we remember the Last Supper in holy Communion, we use this word for the bowl that holds the bread that becomes the Body of Christ. This bowl sometimes looks like a chalice, but the bowl portion is rounder and shallower, and it has a lid to protect the Hosts.

- **Paten** (PAT-en): *Not* called a "plate thingie," this

is the saucer-like disc that holds the bread that becomes the Body of Christ. Often, the altar servers will hold a paten under the chin of the one receiving Communion, keeping particles of or entire Hosts from falling to the ground. Priests, deacons, and EMHCs who visit the sick will carry a Host in a small, round container called a pyx (PICKS).

- **Flagon** (FLAG-on): The bottle or pitcher-like vessel used to hold the wine that will be consecrated at Mass. It is brought forward with the gifts, so it is often kept in the back, to be brought up at the presentation of the gifts.

- **Corporal**: The small, square cloth that the priest spreads out on the altar is the corporal. The sacred vessels used for consecration go on top of it.

- **Purificator**: Exactly as it sounds, this is the napkin-like cloth used to cleanse and purify the chalice after distribution of holy Communion.

- **Pall**: The stiff, square cloth (often there is actually a cardboard square inside to keep it sturdy) that the priest puts over the chalice, ciborium, or paten. Its chief purpose is to keep contaminants (like dust or flies — yes, flies) out of the bread and wine/Body and Blood.

- **Tabernacle**: This is the box- or cabinet-looking thing, often made of gold, where the Blessed

Sacrament is reserved between Masses.

- **Censer and Boat**: Also known as the thurible, the censer contains charcoal and grains of incense, and is used after the offertory to incense the bread and wine, the priest, and congregation. It is also used in the entrance of the priest to Mass. The boat holds the incense until it is added to the charcoal in the censer by the celebrant.

- **Sanctuary Lamp**: This is the oil lamp or wax candle located near the tabernacle, usually red or white. It is always lit whenever the Blessed Sacrament is present, as a sign of honor shown to the Lord. In this way, whenever you enter a church, you will know where the tabernacle or altar is located so that you may genuflect or make a deep bow (see section 60).

- **Monstrance**: This is a large golden or silver vessel that often looks like a sunburst and is usually highly adorned. It holds a consecrated Host for Eucharistic adoration, benediction, and Eucharistic processions.

- **Ambo**: The ambo or pulpit is the place from which the Scripture is proclaimed and the priest preaches. If there is a second podium-like thing in the sanctuary, it is a lectern, usually used for announcements or by the cantor.

BOOKS

- **Roman Missal:** Contains the prayers that are specific to every day's Mass — the opening prayer, prayer over the gifts, prayer after Communion — as well as solemn blessings, Eucharistic prayers, and prefaces for all of the Masses. It's pretty large and recognizable; the altar server often holds it for the priest to read from.

- **Book of the Gospels:** This book contains the Gospel reading for each Sunday of the three-year cycle, plus the Gospels for all of the solemnities, feasts, and other Masses that are celebrated throughout the liturgical year. If it is used, it is often carried in procession by the deacon.

- **Lectionary:** Contains the Scripture readings for Mass (since it has everything, it may be used in place of the Book of the Gospels). It may be carried in the procession by the lector and placed on the ambo.

62

Use your missal (not missile)

When I was a new Catholic, I went to Mass with a cradle Catholic friend. As is natural for all Evangelicals, I brought my Bible to church. He told me, "You don't need that. We have missals."

That's what he said. What I heard was "missiles." "What? Why did he just tell me they have weapons of mass destruction at church?" was all I could think. "Wars and rumors of wars indeed" (Mt 24:6). Jokes aside, I really was confused — until he pulled one out of the pew pocket in front of us and showed me how to use it.

Chances are, you know how the missal works, though the pieces might be in different orders. You'll find the structure of the Mass from the entrance to the final blessing, the Sunday readings and prayers, and hymns. To get the most out of Mass, you should use the missal. You may even find it helpful to get your own, especially if you attend daily Mass. There are several to choose from.

The *Saint Joseph Missal* includes the complete three-year

Sunday Scriptural cycle, including holy day Masses and readings, and common prayers in the back. It also contains a liturgical calendar in the front, and it's accented with full-color illustrations of various biblical scenes, in addition to smaller black-and-white images. This is a good choice for older children who can follow along with the Mass on their own.

The *Saint Paul Missal* is published by the Daughters of St. Paul. It has the Order of the Mass and complete readings and prayers for all Sundays, weekdays, saint feast days, and holy days of obligation. This missal also includes spiritual reflections on the readings. It's a popular choice, and it's usually a high-quality book.

You might also consider subscribing to a monthly publication like *Magnificat*, which includes all Mass readings as well as daily reflections and prayers. If you want a resource for your kids, *Magnificat* offers *Magnifikid*, and there are other children's missals to help toddlers through preteens understand and enjoy the Mass.

Find the right missal for you and your family. While they aren't weapons of mass destruction, they are weapons of Mass instruction.

63

What's the priest wearing?

What we wear says a lot about us. Look around, and you'll soon notice there is always some sort of dress code for particular jobs. It's true for sports, professionals, culinary artists, and laborers. Everyone can distinguish a chef from a construction worker, and a soccer player from a judge. Religion is no different. Look at every religion, and you'll soon notice there is always some sort of dress code, formal or informal, for the clergy.

You may wonder why your priest wears green sometimes and white other times, and then all of a sudden he might be dressed in red (or even pink). There's a good reason for this tradition, as well as for the particular garments that our priests wear. The Office for the Liturgical Celebrations of the Supreme Pontiff puts it best:

> Beyond the historical circumstances, the sacred vestments had an important function in the liturgical celebrations: In the first place, the fact that they are not worn in ordinary life, and thus possess a "liturgical" character, helps one to be detached from the everyday and its concerns

in the celebration of divine worship. Further-more, the ample form of the vestments, the alb, for example, the dalmatic and the chasuble, put the individuality of the one who wears them in second place to emphasize his liturgical role. One might say that the "camouflaging" of the minister's body by the vestments depersonaliz-es him in a way; it is that healthy depersonal-ization that de-centers the celebrating minister and recognizes the true protagonist of the litur-gical action: Christ. The form of the vestments, therefore, says that the liturgy is celebrated "in persona Christi" and not in the priest's own name. He who performs a liturgical function does not do so as a private person, but as a min-ister of the Church and an instrument in the hands of Jesus Christ. The sacred character of the vestments also has to do with their being donned according to what is prescribed in the Roman Ritual.[23]

Here are the standard things you'll see a priest wearing:

- **Clerical collar**: In the Roman rite, you'll usual-ly see your priest in a white clerical collar. This an unmistakable way that the Catholic Church distinguishes her priests and clergy. Sometimes you'll see the shirt color change from the stan-dard black, but the collar is always white.

- **Cassock**: No, your priest is not wearing a dress! The word cassock comes from *casaque*, the French word for the clerical garb that has been in use since the thirteenth century. For certain periods, the garb was the prescribed garment for clergy, and though its use has been relaxed in recent years, many priests still prefer the traditional vestment.

- **Alb**: The alb is a long white linen robe that a priest wears over his regular garments when celebrating Mass. It symbolizes the innocence and purity that should adorn the soul of the priest who ascends the altar. With it comes a long, white, rope-like cord called a *cincture*, which is methodically tied around the waist.

- **Stole**: A stole is a long, thin, scarf-looking piece of fabric that goes around the neck of priests and deacons. The color will reflect the liturgical season or feast day. Notice that both deacons and priests wear stoles, but deacons always wear the stole diagonally from left shoulder to right hip, while priests wear the stole around both shoulders, either crossed in front or with the ends hanging straight down the front. The priest always wears the stole when performing his duties outside of the Mass, such as in the Sacrament of Confession.

- **Chasuble**: Many folks refer to the chasuble simply as the "vestment," but in reality, everything the priest and deacon wear to perform their duties is considered a vestment. Simply put, the chasuble is the large robe that goes over the alb and stole during Mass and benediction services.

The colors on the chasuble and other vestments change with the liturgical season and special feast days. The liturgical colors are:

Green. For Ordinary Time, the time after Epiphany (beginning of January) until Lent and after Pentecost (usually in the beginning of June) until Advent. Why green? It represents the Holy Ghost, life eternal, and hope.

Violet. For the seasons of Advent and Lent, special vigils except for Ascension and Pentecost, and Good Friday. Violet represents penance and humility.

Black. This color is reserved for All Souls' Day and Masses for the dead. Black is for mourning and sorrow.

Rose. It's rose, not pink! Rose represents joy. It is for Gaudete Sunday (the Third Sunday of Advent) and Laetare Sunday (the Fourth Sunday of Lent).

Gold. Also represents joy, and can replace white, red, or green, but not violet or black.

Red. This color represents several things and ideas: the Lord's Passion, blood, fire, God's love, and especially martyrdom. It also represents the Holy Spirit. It is worn on feasts of the Lord's Passion, feasts of the martyrs, Palm Sunday, and Pentecost.

White. For the entire seasons of Christmas and Easter, feasts of the Lord (other than of his Passion), feasts of Mary (Assumption, Immaculate Conception, etc.), the angels, and saints who were not martyrs. It is also worn on All Saints' Day (November 1), feasts of the apostles, nuptial Masses, and funerals or other Masses for the dead. Note that white, rather than black, is always the color worn for children who have died after being baptized without reaching the age of reason.

64

Learn some Latin

Contrary to rumors, Ecclesiastical Latin continues to be the official language of the Roman Catholic Church. The Church still produces official liturgies, canon law, and other publications in Ecclesiastical Latin in order to have a clear and common starting point for all translations.

With that being said, individual parishes and priests have their nuances. Whether it is with the Mass or the prayers they pray, things always vary here and there. One thing I've noticed traveling from parish to parish in the United States and abroad is the use of Latin. Even in the Novus Ordo (English) Mass, I've encountered prayers in Latin that I've never heard before. Countless times I have been at Mass at a new parish, and all of a sudden the priest begins singing one of the parts in Latin. I feel like I'm the only one who doesn't know the lyrics. (This is coming from a person who's been to Mass in Polish, German, Italian, Tajik-Dari, Arabic, and of course in Latin.) No matter the language, it's never fun when you don't know how to join in on the hymns and prayers.

Because of this, I encourage you to memorize prayers, common hymns, and parts of the Mass in Latin. To that end, let's

review some common Latin prayers and parts of the Mass.
Sign of the Cross: We begin with the simplest of them all, also
known as the *Signum Crucis.*

> *In nomine Patris, et Filii, et Spiritus Sancti.*
> *Amen.*

Gloria Patri: This is the "Glory be to the Father" in Latin.

> *Gloria Patri, et Filio, et Spiritui Sancto. Sicut erat*
> *in principio, et nunc, et semper, et in saecula sae-*
> *culorum. Amen.*

Kyrie: This is the penitential "Lord, have mercy" we say in Mass,
and it's actually not Latin, but Greek — the only Greek section
in the Roman rite. Repeated two or three times, depending
on whether you're at the Ordinary Form or the Extraordinary
Form, the petitions are

> *Kyrie eleison, Christe eleison, Kyrie eleison.*

Pater Noster: This is the "Our Father."

> *Pater Noster, qui es in caelis, sanctificetur nomen*
> *tuum. Adveniat regnum tuum. Fiat voluntas tua,*
> *sicut in caelo et in terra. Panem nostrum quotidi-*
> *anum da nobis hodie, et dimitte nobis debita nos-*
> *tra sicut et nos dimittimus debitoribus nostris. Et*
> *ne nos inducas in tentationem, sed libera nos a*
> *malo. Amen.*

Agnus Dei: "*Agnus*" looks a lot like "Angus," a type of beef, but
Agnus means "Lamb." This is the "Lamb of God, you take away

the sins of the world" part of the Mass.

> *Agnus Dei, qui tollis peccata mundi: miserere no-*
> *bis. Agnus Dei, qui tollis peccata mundi: miserere*
> *nobis. Agnus Dei, qui tollis peccata mundi: dona*
> *nobis pacem.*

Sanctus: This is the "Holy, Holy, Holy Lord, God of hosts" prayer we say after the Preface. It goes:

> *Sanctus, Sanctus, Sanctus, Dominus Deus Sa-*
> *baoth, pleni sunt caeli et terra gloria tua. Ho-*
> *sanna in excelsis. Benedictus qui venit in nomine*
> *Domini. Hosanna in excelsis.*

Other Latin prayers you might want to memorize are the Salve Regina and the Ave Maria.

Salve Regina: This is the "Hail, Holy Queen" prayer, which is often said at the end of the Rosary:

> *Salve, Regina, Mater misericordiæ, vita, dulcedo,*
> *et spes nostra, salve. Ad te clamamus exsules filii*
> *Hevæ, Ad te suspiramus, gementes et flentes in*
> *hac lacrimarum valle. Eia, ergo, advocata nostra,*
> *illos tuos misericordes oculos ad nos converte; Et*
> *Jesum, benedictum fructum ventris tui, nobis*
> *post hoc exsilium ostende. O clemens, O pia, O*
> *dulcis Virgo Maria.*

Ave Maria: The Latin "Hail Mary" goes:

> *Ave Maria, gratia plena, Dominus tecum. Ben-*

edicta tu in mulieribus, et benedictus fructus
ventris tui, Iesus. Sancta Maria, Mater Dei, ora
pro nobis peccatoribus, nunc, et in hora mortis
nostrae. Amen.

Being a Modern Catholic

65

Catholic in the modern world

Whether you are seven years old and taking Communion for the first time, or you're a fifty-year-old lifelong Catholic, you will be susceptible to the dangers and pressures of the world.

The modern world offers a host of benefits: medicine and access to resources and information, to name but two. But the modern world, after the developments of philosophical thought of the last three centuries, has turned largely post-Christian, introducing a corruption of morality visible in entertainment, consumer behavior, and health care. Modern Catholics must face this crisis head on. Ask yourself: Are you preparing yourself for this daily battle, or are you sitting back, thinking you know better? It's easy to become lax in judgment, arrogant in knowledge, lazy in prayer, and comfortable with the status quo.

To guard against this, we have to decide carefully what to watch, how to vote, what to read, whom to befriend, and so forth. Together, these contribute to a profound influence in our life. All decisions should be made with prayer. This doesn't mean kneeling each minute of the day with folded hands — being prayerful in all decisions involves intentionality. Do things with the intent of pleasing God. When this is coupled with fervent and heartfelt prayer, excellence in moral judgment will follow.

Catholics, especially in our world today, are faced with many challenges, temptations, and spiritual dangers. It doesn't matter if it's your first or fiftieth Mass homily or confession, or your first or five hundredth video game, party, election ballot, or social media post — you must always be on guard to exercise faithful judgment in what you do, say, consume, and see. Do this with prayer and intentionality, and you will not fail to prevail in charity and morality when dealing with modern issues.

66
Never forget: Evil is real

Early in my teenage years, I enjoyed a reasonably moral decision-making process. No, I wasn't perfect. In various ways, I broke the fourth commandment, but I learned the value of moral judgment and using God's word to calibrate my standards. But when I was fifteen, a friend of mine got his driver's license. He took a few of us on a 9 p.m. drive to the local cemetery, where we walked around. Then my friend led the four of us to his trunk. He reached under a blanket and pulled out a Ouija board.

If you've never heard about this device, it's often referred to as a "talking board." The purpose is to contact the dead. A piece of glass moves around the board through paranormal activity, spelling out words, sharing information, telling fortunes, and providing other information. And I'm going to tell you right now: It works, it is real, and it is evil. That night, we actually learned dead people's names before finding those same names on gravestones, and the dates we asked about for their deaths were consistent with the tombstones, too.

We were just teenagers trying to have a little fun, trying to see if something creepy we'd heard about was in fact real. But my next several years were filled with more sin, more depression, and more self-mutilation than I am willing to explain here. Demons entered into me that day, and it wasn't until I was about twenty years old that many of these behaviors went away after a prebaptism exorcism.

Let's be clear: Satan is real, he wants to corrupt your soul to sever your relationship with God, and he will do anything and use anything to bring you to hell. In my story, the Ouija board was his chosen tool. But notice that the sin of my using that tool was not the only thing harming my soul; an outside influence (in this case, the occult) also manipulated my attitude toward morality. Items, practices, and acceptance of cultural norms have the power to influence us to accept immorality, placing our souls in great peril.

Sin is not linked solely to behavior; it's deeply associated with the things we choose to let influence us. The Ouija board is not farfetched: Hundreds of thousands are in circulation. And many items like these influence us to accept immorality, practice and participate in the occult, or distort the good and authentic teachings of Christianity and the Church.

They include, but definitely are not limited to: astrological readings in the newspaper or online; tarot cards; psychic readings at the fair; gossip disguised as news; pornography and pornographic scenes in television shows and movies; certain spiritual practices disguised as health care, including yoga, Reiki, and the like; and moral relativism.

We must exercise care to avoid these and similar evils. If you are a parent, be concerned to set a good example and to actively teach your children. Evil is real — be on your guard.

67

Combat relativism

"**M**y parents are serious Catholics, but I just don't think Mass is that important." "If you don't want to use contraception because the Church says so, cool. But we think it's okay." "I am personally against abortion, but I believe every woman has a right to choose."

You've undoubtedly heard one of these statements or something similar, and maybe you've even said or thought one of them. This is relativism: the belief that morality is subject to the opinion of each individual. Slowly introduced in the philosophy of René Descartes, Immanuel Kant, and other thinkers, it has gone from a simple idea to an exceedingly popular worldview.

Why is it so popular? Well, it's convenient and easy. The only standard for a person's values and actions is the person's opinions and subjective feelings. Cultural values become irrelevant, and society's ethics and rules of conduct are reduced to personal feelings. Ultimately, relativism destroys religious convictions and morality.

Cardinal Joseph Ratzinger, before he became Pope Benedict XVI, expressed concern about this cancerous moral principle: "Today, having a clear faith based on the Creed of the Church is often labeled as fundamentalism. Whereas relativism, that is, letting oneself be 'tossed here and there, carried about by every wind of doctrine,' seems the only attitude that can cope with modern times. We are building a dictatorship of relativism that does not recognize anything as definitive and whose ultimate goal consists solely of one's ego and desires."[24]

Every Catholic must combat relativism for his or her own soul's benefit and that of society. Refuting relativism first requires that we recognize that some things are absolute, since relativism says, "There are no absolute truths." This claim is self-refuting: To say there are no absolute truths is in itself to assert a truth as absolute. When faced with a relativist, we should try to help them see this simple fact.

Sometimes respectful argument can be helpful. But even more important, we can perform spiritual works of mercy to help those we encounter who espouse a relativistic worldview. The *Catechism of the Catholic Church* (2447) discusses the spiritual works of mercy, which are:

> To instruct the ignorant;
> To counsel the doubtful;
> To admonish sinners;
> To bear wrongs patiently;
> To forgive offenses willingly;
> To comfort the afflicted;
> To pray for the living and the dead.

We shouldn't just say, "That doesn't make sense" and walk away frustrated. Showing mercy includes tactful correction, patience, prayer, forgiveness, and, yes, even comfort for those who exhibit moral relativism. When we are performing these spiritual works, we reflect the character of Christ, the only one who is truly capable of reconciling hearts and minds.

68

Don't believe
everything you hear

Thanks to the internet and digital communications, journalists can publish nearly any story, bloggers can twist quotes or misquote entirely, and folks everywhere can mix up and regurgitate what they hear until the truth is completely lost. The fact is, the truth matters little to many people, and you cannot count on finding truth in many sources you might have trusted at one point in time. As a Catholic, it is important for you to find reliable, balanced, faithful, and truthful resources for your news, commentary, and enjoyment.

I've prided myself on being among the last to be duped by the media frenzies, especially those regarding the Catholic Church and our popes. But in 2017 I became swept up in the news that Pope Francis was ready to change the translation of the Our Father, Christianity's most timeless and recognized prayer. The story went that he thought there was a better translation for "lead us not into temptation" and was going to replace it with a translation similar to the French translation, rendered in English as "do not let us be overcome by temptation." Contrary to most of the made-up scandals of what the pope said (or didn't say) the quotes were correct, even if a little incomplete and without context. Without hesitation, I responded on social media, as did many others. As I later discovered, I had perpetuated a story that wasn't there. Pope Francis was not going to change anything anytime soon. I also lacked context — he had given a homily, commenting on the benefits of the French translation, even mentioning it might be good if we all realized the true meaning of the prayer, but he certainly did not say he was going to change the prayer. It turns out, my comments didn't help Catholics — or anyone else — understand the big picture.

The moral of the story: Don't believe everything you hear when it comes to news of (or even from within!) the Catholic Church. Your best bet when a hot-button issue crops up is to let the dust settle, search however much you have to for direct quotes from the primary sources, and seek commentary from several trusted, orthodox, and reasonable Catholic sources. This isn't to say you cannot think for yourself, but as Catholics we need to be willing to listen to the voices of those who are more fluent in the goings-on of the Church, and who can offer a fresh perspective.

How can you know which sources are "trustworthy"? That's difficult to answer and requires some diligence on your part. In short, the currency of trust is credibility, and for an author or a publication, that is evidenced by years of experience and handling of difficult and complex subjects. Over time, sources like Catholic Answers, Ignatius Press, ETWN, and others have grown to be credible. But you have some homework to complete as well. Always follow these key steps when seeking to discern the truth:

- Know (or seek to learn) what the Church teaches on any given issue, in order to detect falsehoods and red flags.

- Check the credentials of the author.
- Look up the same information from another trusted source to be sure they agree.
- Ask someone with more experience!
- Look up the subject yourself and do some fact finding.

There's another item of importance to cover before we move on, and it gets to the root of the issue: misunderstandings of the Faith and stark anti-Catholicism.

Here's a quote you'll want to remember from Archbishop Fulton Sheen: "There are not over 100 people in this country who hate the Catholic Church. There are, however, millions who hate what they wrongly believe to be the Catholic Church."[25] In other words, the majority of people who speak against the Church do so with little understanding of what Catholicism really is. Bear this in mind when you run into clear lines of bias in the media and elsewhere.

On the other hand, however, we do have to deal with the reality of anti-Catholic bias in the world. The mainstream media often welcomes and encourages anti-Catholic views and rhetoric. This is something we cannot change, but we do not have to let it upset or discourage us. After all, Jesus told us that the world will hate us because it hated him first (Jn 15:18). This means we have all the more reason to educate ourselves and to seek the truth, so we can defend our faith and invite others to understand it, and maybe even to love it as we do.

69

Read *Humanae Vitae*

Signed on July 25, 1968, and released four days later from the Vatican, *Humanae Vitae* is an encyclical from Pope Saint Paul VI on "The Regulation of Births." The document defines the Church's position on the topics of abortion and contraception in cogent prose, leaving no confusion about the urgency of the issue. It also serves as a prophetic warning about the ramifications that are sure to ensue if society ignores or rejects this teaching (both of which have come to pass).

Humanae Vitae uses the term "duty" six times and "responsibility" seventeen times in its brief discourse. When the Church uses the terms "duty" and "responsibility" to inform Catholics of a particular matter, we should be attentive: This is an extraordinary matter of faith and morals.

Notably, the text explicitly states the Church's opposition to the use of contraception and the practice of abortion. Unfortunately, a Pew Research Center report in 2016 found that among modern American Catholics, just 8 percent said contraception is morally wrong, with 89 percent saying it is either morally acceptable or not a moral issue at all. This same report found that about one in ten (13 percent) of Catholics who attend Mass weekly said contraception is morally wrong, with 87 percent saying it is either acceptable or not a moral issue.[26]

I need to say this plainly: This is a crisis. We must acknowledge three facts: (1) *Humanae Vitae* expresses the definite position of the Church; (2) the teachings expressed in it will not change; and (3) the problems it outlines are not going away anytime soon. Wherever you currently stand on these issues, I urge you to read *Humanae Vitae* thoughtfully and attentively.

Marriage, contraception, and abortion are among the most politically and morally divisive issues in the modern world, and reading *Humanae Vitae* will solidify your understanding of these critical topics. By reading this document, you'll be equipped to answer questions about the Church's teaching on marital love and responsible parenthood, as well as to affirm traditional Church moral teaching on the sanctity of life and the procreative and unitive nature of conjugal relations. In short, you'll know more about sex, birth, and marriage in a context that's relevant to the modern Catholic.

But don't just read *Humanae Vitae*. Believe it, share it, and defend it, in light of what Pope Saint Pius V once said: "All the evils in the world are due to lukewarm Catholics." The Catholic Church is the longest-lasting, largest, and most successful institution the world has ever seen. The Catholic Church will never go away, and she will never alter her moral and dogmatic teaching because that teaching is truth. Because of these facts, the whole world will continue to look toward this one, holy, catholic, and apostolic faith for answers to the hardest questions. It behooves us, then, to share and defend these teachings of extraordinary importance. The fabric and survival of our society literally depend on it.

70

The truth about contraception

My wife and I used birth control for years, and I regret it terribly.[27] My non-Catholic pastor was silent on birth control from the pulpit, so I thought the idea of preventing pregnancy through contraception was morally acceptable. I convinced my wife to get on the pill, the shot, and the patch early in our marriage. It was a fiasco from the beginning, and I should have known when to read the writing on the wall: My wife suffered quite a bit: gaining weight, harming her immune system, and struggling with mood swings. I also ignored my own guilt for postponing children just so I could finish a degree.

Years later, we became Catholic, and during that time we were pregnant with our first child, Gabriel. We weren't on birth control any longer, but not because we believed it was sinful: We just wanted a baby. Soon, at the suggestion of my deacon, I read *Humanae Vitae*. The document confused me when it described the concept of responsible parenthood. All I could think was, "If I'm not a parent — at least, not yet — why should I care?" My confusion rested in my faulty understanding of the responsibilities I had to God and to my spouse in the Sacrament of Matrimony.

Humanae Vitae states: "Responsible parenthood also and above all implies a more profound relationship to the objective moral order established by God, of which a right conscience is the faithful interpreter. The responsible exercise of parenthood implies, therefore, that husband and wife recognize their own duties fully toward God, toward themselves, toward the family and toward society, in a correct hierarchy of values."[28]

Paul VI is saying here that the act of intentionally thwarting the procreative end of our sexuality is wrong because it's a conscious violation of God's design for us. The pleasures that intercourse provides are added blessings from God, strengthening the bond of intimacy, respect, and love between husband and wife, while at the same time offering the possibility of creating a new life. The Church sees the two ends of the marital act (unity and procreation) as completely inseparable. It is not either/or, but always both/and. It doesn't matter if pregnancy is unlikely or impossible in a particular instance; the essence of the sexual act remains the same.

When we look at the big picture of marriage and sex, the loving environment that is created by the marital act is the perfect setting for nurturing and educating children. But if sexual pleasure within marriage becomes unnatural or is at odds with how God intended it, it is harmful to the whole family.

There is one instance in which contraceptives are not strictly immoral: if you have a severe, life-threatening condition. If you believe this is the case, consult your priest.

But does the Catholic Church expect married couples to produce children immediately upon being fertile, and endlessly so from then on? Of course not. The Church promotes family-planning practices that agree with the natural rhythms of a body's fertility. Many Catholic couples choose Natural Family

Planning (NFP) as a means of effectively planning childbirth at times that are best for their family.

Some mistakenly believe that NFP is simply "Catholic birth control." That couldn't be further from the truth, because birth control actively engages unnatural hormones designed to prevent pregnancy (even going so far as destroying sperm). NFP actually doesn't prevent pregnancy; it simply allows you to know when the woman's body is fertile so you can abstain from sex at those times. The arguments against NFP are dead on arrival — be assured that it is a safe and moral choice for married couples.

71

Save sex for marriage

Story time. I was sexually active before I was married. No, not with my wife. Know what I mean? A day came when I saw what belonged to the world, and I realized I needed a deep and heartfelt change in my lifestyle and relationship choices if I wanted to be married one day. Let me rephrase that: if I wanted to remain married one day to a wonderful, faithful woman. I wanted to give my future wife absolutely no doubt that it was only God, and only her, that I cared about. It wasn't easy, but I swore off sex. I swore off kissing. I swore off dating until I was prayerfully engaged with a woman. It eventually came around. My future wife entered my life, and I explained my past, my expectations of myself, and what I wanted in a relationship and marriage. The rest is history — but that choice to be chaste, I believe, was a critical ingredient to the enjoyable and productive marriage we've had for over ten years.

Saint John Henry Newman remarked, "Virtue is its own reward, and brings with it the truest and highest pleasure." Chastity, while not a cardinal virtue, is no different. Chastity applies to all of us, in all states of life. For unmarried Catholics, it means refraining from sexual activity. This is not a negative restriction, but a helpful guard against shame, heartbreak, and much unnecessary suffering. Among the most significant benefits are trust, communication, and commitment — keys to a happy and fruitful marriage.

When we save sex for marriage, we gain trust that the intentions of the other person match our own. We never have to worry about underlying motives within a relationship if an object like sex is not a consolation prize. Chastity also fosters communication. Perhaps contrary to some people's belief, couples who wait on their way to the altar talk a lot about sex — what their expectations are, what fears they have, what is morally incorrect — and they establish several boundaries that build unity, love, and pleasure when the time will be right to share in the marital act. Everyone yearns for commitment. This heavily affects and is affected by trust, the first benefit mentioned. Couples who wait know, beyond any doubt, that there was intimacy within the relationship well prior to the introduction of sexual intimacy. Pope Saint John Paul II's words are highly needed in our times: "Only the chaste man and the chaste woman are capable of real love."

If you're engaged, or even if you're not, and you haven't yet addressed this topic between you and the Lord, do it now: Commit to chastity and celibacy. The rewards are unspeakable. You'll enrich your relationship with meaning; you'll receive the passion in lovemaking that you desire; and you'll gain lifelong trust from a spouse who loves you, trusts you, and wants to give themselves to you in return. Not to mention, you'll be more attentive to the direction that God is leading you, which might not be married life after all. He might want you all to himself as a priest or religious.

72

What the Church teaches about homosexuality

Catholic morality calls homosexual acts sinful. Note well, the Church does not call people with homosexual tendencies evil (far from it), but only the acts themselves. It would be easy to end the topic there, but the issue is deeper than that. The culture at large demands a calculated response when it says — often as a systematic slogan — that homosexuals are "born that way," and we must simply accept their state of life, changing our laws and the way we view morality in order to protect and respect them.

The *Catechism* lays out the basis of the Church's teaching against homosexual acts:

> Homosexuality refers to relations between men or between women who experience an exclusive or predominant sexual attraction toward persons of the same sex. It has taken a great variety of forms through the centuries and in different cultures. Its psychological genesis re-

mains largely unexplained. Basing itself on Sacred Scripture, which presents homosexual acts as acts of grave depravity, tradition has always declared that "homosexual acts are intrinsically disordered." They are contrary to the natural law. They close the sexual act to the gift of life. They do not proceed from a genuine affective and sexual complementarity. Under no circumstances can they be approved. (2357)

Regarding same-sex attraction, the *Catechism* states, "The number of men and women who have deep-seated homosexual tendencies is not negligible. This inclination, which is objectively disordered, constitutes for most of them a trial" (2358).

The Church recognizes that same-sex attractions can be very painful for a person, but she also teaches clearly that these attractions are "objectively disordered." They are a violation of the natural law and the Church's moral Magisterium.

But once again, the conversation does not stop there. Our duty as Christians is not to hold signage condemning sin, but to love sinners as Christ did, regardless of their habits or state of life. The Church's conversation on homosexuals confirms that they must be accepted with respect, compassion, and sensitivity, and that any sign of unjust discrimination in their regard should be avoided. We as Catholics believe that those with homosexual inclinations are called to fulfill God's will in their lives, to allow him to convert their hearts, and to unite to the sacrifice of the Lord's cross the difficulties they may encounter from their condition (CCC 2358). Still, acceptance of a person does not equate to acceptance of their inclinations or sins.

A related topic is so-called same-sex marriage. I say "so-called" because these same-sex unions are not in fact marriage and should not be given that label. Why? Because of what marriage is: a covenant between a man and a woman, in which they "establish between themselves a partnership of the whole of life" (CCC 1601). Marriage, to the Church, is immutable: It cannot change from what it is, and any deviation from what it is would make it something else. Why? Because God, not humans, made marriage.

Marriage was made by God for man and woman to enjoy as pleasure and to take on as a responsibility. The *Catechism* states, "The intimate community of life and love which constitutes the married state has been established by the Creator and endowed by him with its own proper laws. ... God himself is the author of marriage" (1603). Because of its dignity, marriage has been raised to a sacrament by Jesus Christ. All generations of Catholics must rise up and protect marriage under these terms. Since we are children of God, marriage is ours to defend as a most gracious inheritance and responsibility.

73

Break free from masturbation and pornography

Pornography is a serious problem in our society, and even in our Church. Some studies report that as many as half of all Christian men are addicted to (or have experienced addiction to) pornography. Other surveys suggest four out of every five Catholic men confess the sin of viewing pornography, which is almost always associated with masturbation. Pew surveys about confession might or might not represent the full truth, but the oversexualization of our modern time cannot be ignored and cannot be denied. Men face, now more than ever, a daunting course to holiness.

The problem is most frequent with boys and men, but women also struggle with addiction to pornography in increasing numbers. Many adults — especially adult men — still suffer from early decisions to look at porn and masturbate without any understanding of the chains they were forging for themselves. And thus we have today many Christian men who want holiness, but who suffer from addiction. Maybe you find yourself in this situation right now. Do not despair! God's grace is stronger than any addiction or sin. But you do have some hard work to do. Even if you've tried thousands of times to quit, made numerous declarations, and confessed endlessly without any result, have hope. There are resources available to you. Here's the game plan:

- **Get professional help.** If you have tried endlessly to quit and been unsuccessful, it is likely you are addicted. You need to seek professional help to combat the addiction. It's important to understand that addiction is a disease, and like any other disease (physical or mental), it requires professional guidance to root it out and cure it. Find a licensed therapist who specializes in the treatment of sex addictions. For more information on faith-based treatments, check out resources like IntegrityRestored.com.

- **Practice a sacramental lifestyle.** Go to confession regularly — even once a week, if necessary. Confession (see sections 10 and 11) is the most effective means of correcting sinful behavior. Harness your shame to produce holiness. Get a personal confessor, someone who can hear your confession regularly. This provides accountability, and a good confessor will also provide you with the advice and spiritual support you need. The make-or-break key to this, though, is honesty. You have to tell the truth, or you will only be hurting your progress and adding the sin of lying.

- **Get further accountability**. Have your spouse or a good friend set up accountability software (like Covenant Eyes) and parental controls on your media devices — all of them. From your PlayStation to your Kindle, you need to get rid of the sources, and precautions will significantly aid you.

- **Pray**. I especially recommend praying the Rosary. Prayer is a priority. If you're not actively engaged in prayer to battle porn, you need to be. I suggest the Rosary because it's Our Lady's prayer, and she is the queen of purity. You cannot reasonably pray the whole Rosary every day and also look at porn. Let the Rosary be your weapon.

- **Read about hell**. I mean it. Shame leads us to fear getting caught and facing negative consequences for misbehavior. But sometimes to kick out big sins, we need more than shame—we need healthy fear of sin's consequences. When it comes to sin, God knows every time, and masturbation and pornography are always grave matters. (Remember, a sin is mortal if it involves grave matter, full knowledge, and deliberate consent.) Every mortal sin separates us from God. Sometimes we need to seek a proper sense of what the torments of hell will be like, because we want motivation to not go there. Read a book about the visions of Fátima, the very brief *Hell and Its Torments* by Saint Robert Bellarmine, or other spiritual reading. If it helps you remove these sins from your life, it's okay to be motivated, for a time, by fear of punishment.

As you set out to remove pornography and any other unchaste ways of living from your life, I want to leave you with encouragement: Always, always, always have hope. Arm yourself with God's promises:

- "Have I not commanded you? Be strong and of good courage; be not frightened, neither be dismayed; for the Lord your God is with you wherever you go." (Joshua 1:9)

- "Fear not, for I am with you, be not dismayed, for I am your God; I will strengthen you, I will help you, I will uphold you with my victorious right hand." (Isaiah 41:10)

- "Cast your burden on the Lord, and he will sustain you; he will never permit the righteous to be moved." (Psalm 55:22)

- "No temptation has overtaken you that is not common to man. God is faithful, and he will not let you be tempted beyond your strength, but with the temptation will also provide the way of escape, that you may be able to endure it." (1 Corinthians 10:13)

- "For you know that the testing of your faith produces steadfastness." (James 1:3)

- "Blessed is the man who endures trial, for when

he has stood the test he will receive the crown of life which God has promised to those who love him." (James 1:12)

Don't ever give up this fight. Be sure to help others who are struggling by encouraging them and being available to them as an accountability partner.

74

Teach your kids about healthy sexuality

The war for chastity is fought on two fronts: the individual's struggle for their own personal holiness and the parents' battle for their kids' souls. The chances are high that by eleven years old, most boys (and many girls, also) will have seen their first pornographic image.

The most effective means of defeating porn and keeping people safe from addiction is to catch it early. This means parents must assume their proper role and responsibility in the sexual formation of their children. Since our culture doesn't do so, we need to educate children from an early age about human dignity. A hundred years ago, this might not have been the case, but the rapid oversexualization of our youth has made this something Catholic parents now have to address.

A father's example is the most meaningful and effective formation of a young man's sexual views, and it's drastically important for young women, too. A six-year-old doesn't need to study Theology of the Body to understand the concepts behind the objectification of women. He can learn this first and foremost by naturally observing the way his dad treats other women: how he treats Mom, the sorts of movies he watches, the jokes he might tell (or laugh at), the nicknames or labels he uses for women, the things he lets his boy get away with, and so on.

Active teaching should take place, also. Parents can approach the topic of sexuality from several angles. Discuss the Super Bowl ad you didn't mean for your kids to see; encourage proper and modest dress; explain how to treat siblings and friends of the opposite sex; make sure they understand their own innate human dignity. Most importantly, parents should regularly discuss and monitor their kids' media habits. This isn't spying; it's accountability. It is possible, though difficult, to craft a wholesome, agreeable, and productive relationship between parents and children that allows the child to truly seek the good of himself and others.

I also recommend that you set up accountability software (like Covenant Eyes) and parental controls on every media device in your home, from smart phones to PlayStations.

Finally, it's important to pray — often — for chastity in your home and for each of your children. These are broad examples, but we as parents must make a consistent effort to ensure our children understand the value and proper place of sexuality. If we do not take an active role in talking to our kids about sex and morality, someone else will. Even the most well-intentioned and engaged children will be tempted to discover the possibilities of their bodies, so it's critical that we give them knowledge and tools to conquer temptations.

75

Know how to respond to abuse scandals

There are two things you need to know about abuse in the Church: It's nothing new, and it brings shame on the entire Church. It's unequivocally unacceptable.

No matter what someone tells you, abuse in the Church is nothing new. Beginning with Judas Iscariot, one of Jesus' chosen Twelve, the abuse of power, position, and influence has been a problem. Judas used his power, position, and influence to betray the Son of Man. Later, consecrated bishops like Arius used their power as a means of gaining political clout, to push a heretical ideology on masses of priests, laity, and secular rulers. Cardinals, popes, and all levels of clergy from the late Middle Ages to the Counter-Reformation used their offices for financial gain, political power, and corruption. Today in our Church, we are facing the crisis of sexual abuse and cover-up.

Sadly, abuse is always, on some level, a concern, which means abuse, on some level, is not going away. There will always be usurpers of power, users of influence, and exploiters of position.

This does not mean that abuse is something we simply accept. Yes, sin is a reality; but sin is also never acceptable. How, then, do we best deal with scandal when it happens? It is, above all, important to have an appropriate and effective mindset, and to employ a reasonable reaction.

The natural response to abuse is similar to that of grief. Grief is the multifaceted emotional response to loss. The loss that occurs during every abuse scandal is a loss of faith in leadership, a loss of confidence in the Church's structure, and a loss of sureness of the veracity of the Church. Scandals are like viruses, with the power to cripple the Body of Christ.

But abuses in the Church induce more than grief. Some faithful suffer anxiety. Some encounter emotional torment or persecution. Some become (or remain) bitter. Others lose trust, almost permanently. Long past the anger of grief and bitterness, they associate clerical responsibility with innate sinfulness. Each of these causes a state of fear, which leads to a lack of spiritual growth and evangelical productivity.

How do we respond to abuse scandals without anxiety, bitterness, permanent distrust, and the host of other negative responses? Every sin needs to be uprooted, and every scandal needs to be dealt with. But scandals, like sins, cannot be uprooted and vanquished until they are identified and made publicly visible. While this is deeply painful, it is also an opportunity for all of us to be vigilant and work hard to ensure that the same sins don't happen again.

Our first priority is to hold people accountable for their actions, as well as their inactions. Accountability is everyone's job, and it gives the faithful the opportunity to demand better from our leaders and to demand better leaders, period.

Next, we should recognize the ways in which God is using the scandals to increase our faith. Remember, God can bring great good out of the most terrible evils. The realization of sin leads us to realize our need for a savior; and knowing our Savior is just as important as knowing how much we need him.

PREPARING FOR AN ABUSE SCANDAL

Because we know that scandals will come, it's important for us to anticipate scandal in the Church. The pope said this, a priest did that, this bishop knew something and covered it up, a group of seminarians knew for years and said nothing — we've seen the headlines. As I pointed out in the previous section, abuse has arisen countless times in our Church's history. Each member of the Church is still fallen and still prone to sin, and even our shepherds are not exempt.

There's a saying I've heard: "You don't leave Jesus because of Judas." Well, you don't leave Peter because of Judas either. The Church is a body: You don't cut off your hand just because you lost feeling in your finger. You don't abandon your head and heart because you lost your vision.

The best way to prepare for a scandal is to know exactly what you believe in, and why. We don't believe in the Eucharist because others told us to; we believe because the God of the universe told us he is there. We don't believe in Jesus because he was a nice guy; we believe that he is God because he proved it by healing the sick, raising people from the grave, and defeating death after dying as a perfect sacrifice himself.

Here's the bottom line: You don't believe in the Church because her people are perfect, because they're not. You believe in the Church because her head is perfect.

When you know what you believe in, and why, you're an immovable fortress against scandal. Nothing that ever happens can alter the truth that the Catholic Church professes. Nothing. It is more important to continue believing and working out our own sanctity and salvation (see Phil 2:12) than to let the sins of others cause us to despair.

What specific actions can we laypeople take when abuse scandals shake our Church? Aside from holding our leaders accountable and praying, we also need to offer penance. It can seem counterintuitive and even unfair to suffer for the sins of others, yet this is our calling as followers of Christ, our sinless leader, who suffered for the sins of the whole world. One place this kind of corporate accountability exists is in the military, where, when one person gets in trouble, everyone gets in trouble. As a veteran, I can tell you that that fact is awful sometimes, but it serves two critical ends: better accountability and more responsible soldiers.

As Catholics, we know that our corporal and spiritual works may obtain graces that benefit others. We also believe that we can bear sufferings or do works that help make satisfaction for sin, both sins we commit and the sins of the world. Saint Paul refers to this concept in Colossians 1:24 when he declares, "Now I rejoice in my sufferings for your sake, and in my flesh I complete what is lacking in Christ's afflictions for the sake of his body, that is, the church." Just as we do penance as individuals, we should seek penance as a whole Church.

Here are some ways you can make this part of your life, especially in your family:

- Pray the Rosary — and, if you have a family, pray the Rosary as a family.
- Practice a Friday penance by abstaining from eating meat and adding another act of fasting (e.g., refraining from another form of food or drink, skipping a meal, or giving up television).
- Spend an hour of adoration before the Blessed Sacrament.
- Pray the Divine Mercy chaplet — again, as a family, if possible.

How you will react to an abuse scandal is up to you, but the one thing that will help the future of the Body of Christ is offering up your suffering for the benefit of others. When one person sins, it affects us all. Yet Scripture reassures us that "where sin increased, grace abounded all the more" (Rom 5:12). We can be sure that when one person does penance, it is effective for all.

76

Speak out against abortion

The people of God have continually preached against the evils of abortion. The Christian faith emerges from the faith of God's chosen people, the Hebrews, and they, too, have always defended the sanctity of life in the womb. In the Mosaic Law, the "eye for an eye" teaching deals with this directly: "When men strive [or, "fight"] together, and hurt a woman with child, so that there is a miscarriage [or, "so that her child comes out"], and yet no harm follows, the one who hurt her shall be fined, according as the woman's husband shall lay upon him; and he shall pay as the judges determine. If any harm follows, then you shall give life for life, eye for eye, tooth for tooth, hand for hand, foot for foot" (Ex 21:22–24).

Christian teaching has consistently fought for the rights of the unborn and against abortion. *The Didache*, an early catechism of morality written around the year A.D. 70, says of abortion: "You shall not procure [an] abortion, nor destroy a newborn child."[29]

In the second century, Tertullian wrote: "In our case, a murder being once for all forbidden, we may not destroy even the fetus in the womb, while as yet the human being derives blood from the other parts of the body for its sustenance. To hinder a birth is merely a speedier man-killing; nor does it matter whether you take away a life that is born, or destroy one that is coming to birth. That is a man which is going to be one; you have the fruit already in its seed."[30]

Most of the Church Fathers also wrote on the Church's position on abortion, and all were unanimously against it as an evil equivalent to murder.

Yet, the evil of abortion not only still exists today, it is commonplace. As Catholics, we are called to stand up to defend innocent lives. As soon as you attempt to do this, you'll encounter arguments. Typically, there are three common arguments in defense of abortion. Let's look at how to defend the pro-life position confidently, reasonably, and charitably.

THE WOMAN'S BODY

In this first argument, the usual statement goes, "Her body, her choice." The logic here is that a woman has the right to decide what she can and can't do with her body; the fetus is part of her body; she has the right to determine whether the fetus remains in her body, which means she has the right to abort the fetus if she wants.

Depending on who you're talking to, there are two main ways to approach this. First, a basic understanding of genetics proves the foundational assertion of this argument wrong. The DNA a mother has is wholly different from the new DNA, which constitutes a separate person in the womb.

Second, there is the slightly more philosophical "Transitive Possession of Body Parts" argument. If A is part of B and B is part of C, then necessarily, A must be part of C. This is called a transitive relation, and it's what the pro-abortion argument here is based on. Yet we need to consider that the unborn baby is also composed of parts. At eight weeks after conception, all the major body parts are present (even if not yet functioning). Now, if the unborn has parts and the unborn is itself a part of the mother, then the parts of the unborn would also have to be called parts of the mother. But this leads to logical absurdities. How many feet does a mother have at, say, twelve weeks gestation? Two or four? If we assume that the unborn is a part of the mother, then we would have to answer four. We would also have to say that she has a penis if she's pregnant with a boy, but this is absurd.

The woman's body is where the fetus is located, not what the fetus is. In other words, the unborn baby is not part of its mother's body. When a baby is created, it is a new person. It has its own heartbeat, its own organs, and its own soul, which gives it movement. Because it is a whole separate person, the woman does not get to decide what happens to this innocent new life.

WOMEN WILL DIE OF UNSAFE ABORTIONS IF WE MAKE ALL ABORTIONS ILLEGAL

This position is flawed because it does not follow its own end. Is it a good idea to legislate the killing of children in the womb because people will kill their children anyway? The only logical answer is "no"! Should rape be legalized so that the government can make it safer and cleaner? Or murder, because people will do it anyway? Nowhere else is this logic applied than to abortion, and it proves itself wrong.

It is also a myth. Before *Roe v. Wade*, most illegal abortions were already happening in clean, monitored, sanitary doctor's offices by trained and experienced physicians (see EWTN's *Pro-life Encyclopedia*).

WOMEN WHO ARE RAPED SHOULDN'T HAVE TO CARRY A CHILD

This is a deeply sensitive subject. Rape is uniquely evil, and the victims of rape suffer so much more beyond the pregnancy forced upon them. Victims suffer from tremendous pain, torment, and emotional damage, and many rape victims never fully recover from the trauma. We cannot be calloused to this grave evil.

The reality is that abortion does not assist a woman in finding healing after rape. In fact, abortion can make the pain of rape significantly harder to bear. Advocates of abortion don't realize, especially if they have never had one, the indescribable agony of regret that is the inevitable result. If the consequences of rape and abortion are compounded, this is usually catastrophic for a woman, sometimes leading to suicide.

What is the answer then? Rape is a crime, which merits the just punishment of the criminal. But extending that punishment to an innocent child, who is also a victim, is unjust. The child did not elect to be conceived this way, but that does not mean its life should be ended. Above all, that child is a victim and needs to be defended also. Abortion merely adds trauma to trauma.

These are just three common arguments to support abortion. While it's important to have some talking points to respond to these arguments, the most important thing is to become a pro-life advocate however you can, no matter the cost. The topic of abortion is not going away unless we continue to march, speak, and actively defend the unborn. The unborn cannot save themselves. There have been an estimated 60 million abortions since *Roe v. Wade*, the extermination of half a generation.[31] The Centers for Disease Control and Prevention (CDC) reported 652,000 abortions in 2014 alone.[32] The war for the unborn is not a matter of winning arguments. Instead, we must fight with our minds and words to change the culture and legislation, to save the lives of countless babies who have nobody else to advocate for them.

77

What the Church teaches about euthanasia

The steady creep of individualistic philosophies in Western culture over the last three centuries has produced arguments for relativism, reversing well-established Christian moral teaching on topics having to do with life and death. And euthanasia is at the forefront of these issues we deal with today.

Here's a common situation: A man receives news that he has cancer. Optimistic at first, he engages in medical treatment, but he soon realizes fighting cancer is going to be the most difficult undertaking of his life. To make matters worse, there's no guarantee that the disease won't return, and at some point he'll have to pay for chemotherapy. Then he discovers that some states have legalized assisted suicide. He has been told his illness is terminal. Feeling empowered by his new option, he is convinced he would rather "go out his own way." He sees more dignity choosing his own way of dying, "facing death on his own terms," rather than letting an illness kill him at its own speed.

Consider this real-life headline: In the late 1980s, Nancy Cruzan had been in a coma for nearly eight years, but she wasn't dying, and her body was showing zero signs of deterioration. After some arguments were presented defending her "right to die," the courts allowed food and water to be discontinued. Twelve days later, she died, right after Christmas. Nancy did not die of the coma but of starvation, at thirty-three years old. Yet it was called a "merciful death." This landmark case set the standard for common-law interpretations relating to end-of-life law and litigation.

The push for euthanasia is the result of corrupted understanding of rights, and a refusal to acknowledge the value of suffering. There is also a disregard for the sanctity of human life, since those who believe in euthanasia think that some good can come from ending a life. These moral viewpoints are the reasons doctors recommend terminating pregnancies of abnormal fetuses and ending the lives of elderly men and women with dementia, and any other members of society who are considered undesirable.

How does the Catholic Church respond? The Congregation for the Doctrine of the Faith made a declaration on euthanasia in 1980, defining the issue and discussing the numerous factors contributing to the moral problem. The document is almost forty years old, yet it still answers every argument presented in our time.

The Congregation clarifies that, as Catholics, we don't simply believe life is sacred and nondisposable. Rather, it is a gift of God's love. Therefore, when someone chooses to take their own life, regardless of the conditions, their choice is firstly a direct and grave attack on God's love for that person.

The Church is not pitiless, though; she recognizes the anguish in suffering and the pain of moments in life where suffering appears to be useless. The Church even prescribes, with a warning of the moderation that must be applied, the use of painkillers and medical solutions to reduce suffering. But suffering is a central issue in Christian theology. After all, the word "passion" means struggle, or suffering, and there is no better passion to consider unjust than that of Jesus Christ. The Congregation states:

> According to Christian teaching, suffering, especially suffering during the last moments of life, has a special place in God's saving plan; it is in fact a sharing in Christ's passion and a union with the redeeming sacrifice which he offered in obedience to the Father's will. Therefore, one must not be surprised if some Christians prefer to … accept voluntarily at least a part of their sufferings and thus associate themselves in a conscious way with the sufferings of Christ crucified.[33]

The matter of euthanasia corresponds closely to the dignity and very concept of life. Catholics consider every life valuable not by its contribution to society, but by its very existence, since that existence is proof of God's love. Protecting life is a duty that involves defending the love of God. The only true "right to die" is the right of dying peacefully with human and Christian dignity. Catholics share this hope because we know that death is not the end; it's the doorway to eternal life. When we look at human life as a whole through this lens, it becomes apparent that our whole life is a preparation for death. We should accept this unavoidable truth with responsibility and true dignity.

78

The Church's stance on immigration

One of the most significant issues in the world — not just the United States — is the issue of immigration. In fact, it's been a concern since antiquity, from the Etruscans and the Romans to the refugee and illegal immigrant crises of the modern day. Leaving aside the political aspects, what the Catholic Church's social Magisterium teaches about immigration should be adequately understood by all Catholics.

The highlights of the Church's position can be found in the *Catechism of the Catholic Church*:

> The more prosperous nations are obliged, to the extent they are able, to welcome the *foreigner* in search of the security and the means of livelihood which he cannot find in his country of origin. Public authorities should see to it that the natural right is respected that places a guest under the protection of those who receive him.
>
> Political authorities, for the sake of the

common good for which they are responsible, may make the exercise of the right to immigrate subject to various juridical conditions, especially with regard to the immigrants' duties toward their country of adoption. Immigrants are obliged to respect with gratitude the material and spiritual heritage of the country that receives them, to obey its laws and to assist in carrying civic burdens. (2241)

Another resource for understanding the Church's social teaching on immigration is the 1963 encyclical from Pope Saint John XXIII, *Pacem in Terris* (Peace on Earth). His points on the rights inherent in immigration are particularly important:

- On the right to emigrate and immigrate: "Again, every human being has the right to freedom of movement and of residence within the confines of his own State. When there are just reasons in favor of it, he must be permitted to emigrate to other countries and take up residence there. The fact that he is a citizen of a particular State does not deprive him of membership in the human family, nor of citizenship in that universal society, the common, world-wide fellowship of men."[34]

- On the rights of refugees: "It is not irrelevant to draw the attention of the world to the fact that these refugees are persons and all their rights as persons must be recognized. Refugees cannot lose these rights simply because they are deprived of citizenship of their own States. And among man's personal rights we must include his right to enter a country in which he hopes to be able to provide more fittingly for himself and his dependents. It is therefore the duty of State officials to accept such immigrants and — so far as the good of their own community, rightly understood, permits — to further the aims of those who may wish to become members of a new society."[35]

The Church is always at the forefront of the culture and subculture, so you can be absolutely assured that this institution, which has remained intact for two thousand years, has a firm grip on the social and human implications regarding immigration. As these topics develop and become part of everyday headlines, look to the Church with trust in her wisdom on immigration.

79
Stop gossiping

A toxic problem of everyday life in the modern world is gossip. Most people agree that gossip is bad for everyone; Christians who remember the eighth commandment shouldn't need to be told that this is so. As Catholics, we need to avoid gossip and develop a sense of self-awareness to detect when the temptation to gossip approaches. "No one is bound to reveal the truth to someone who does not have the right to know it," says the *Catechism* (2489). That's where we should draw the line.

Water-cooler details about the way so-and-so talks to the boss, or chatter in the narthex about that couple who wears shorts and flip-flops to Mass, are frequent occasions of gossip. More severe examples of gossip are sharing secrets that might damage a person's reputation, or planting seeds of doubt about a person's intentions without relevant facts or appreciation for the circumstances. Passive gossip exists, too, in the content in magazines and articles we share online, when the content of that information is slanderous or libelous. Even clicking that "like" button on social media perpetuates the dissemination of information when it's gossip. But gossip isn't just toxic for the workplace or other social environments; what seems like idle scuttlebutt is a toxin to our souls.

It's incredibly easy to gossip without even realizing it, but there remain sure ways to combat this pernicious sin. The most obvious solution is to avoid and back off from conversations where gossip is already occurring. What started out as a simple chat quickly devolved into a gripe session about a specific individual. Sound familiar? Identify this immediately, and if you can't change the subject, walk away.

Maybe you need to be around; since you cannot leave, why not change the subject? Sometimes, changing gears and sticking to the healthy subject that was originally up for discussion is a tactic everyone present can appreciate. And you know what? A simple joke lightens the mood, too — but don't make the joke about the person involved in the gossip. Another way to derail gossip is to offer a positive or fresh perspective. Is a friend always showing up late to events? Does your priest always forget what a reasonable time for a confession is? Is your boss digging into the weeds on a project you're paying skillful attention to? Don't fret — avoid that gossip by rephrasing your observation with a positive perspective. It's more than a spin if it's also the truth!

Another solid tactic to avoid gossip is to — politely — point it out in your common groups of friends if it's an issue. When you do this the right way, the result is a cool disarming of the one(s) sharing information, not looking like a judge-y friend whom nobody can trust or share information with.

Gossip is a sin of the tongue, and it can be very serious. Our speech is capable of much damage: spreading hate; telling lies; sharing misinformation or errors; causing discouragement, fear, or despair. At its core, it's a sin against justice. The Church offers a solid means of correcting this:

> Every offense committed against justice and truth entails the *duty of reparation*, even if its

author has been forgiven. ... If someone who has suffered harm cannot be directly compensated [e.g., if he is long dead], he must be given moral satisfaction in the name of charity. This duty of reparation also concerns offenses against another's reputation. This reparation, moral and sometimes material, must be evaluated in terms of the extent of the damage inflicted. It obliges in conscience. (CCC 2487)

To put it plainly, make the situation right. In most cases, the destruction of gossip can be undone through a meaningful apology and a retraction of the information shared.

80

Give, and give out of love

As a Catholic, it us up to you and your fellow parishioners to be sure your parish is adequately funded. We have a responsibility to give financially to our church, according to our ability.

Ever paid your electric bill or your heating bill in the middle of the winter and balked at the figures? Imagine running a parish that's 10,000–30,000 square feet. Often, the parish has difficulty just meeting the electric bill because of the lack of donations and tithing. According to a study, the median income across the United States for Catholics is 5 percent more than other Christian denominations.[36] Catholics can give more than we actually do, and we should. This is called tithing.

The standard rule of thumb for tithing is 10 percent of your income. Where does this standard come from? The Bible does not say that Christians must tithe 10 percent. In the Old Testament, the Law required the Hebrews to "tithe all the yield of your seed, which comes forth from the field year by year" (Dt 14:22). This was a Mosaic law, but Christ fulfilled this law (Mt 5:17) and Christians are not bound to it.

So, what gives? If Christians are not required to tithe, can't we just forget it? The answer is no, because Christians are bound by the law of the New Covenant: the Law of Love. The Mosaic Law was, essentially, the minimum. Its purpose, according to Saint Paul, was to point us to Christ, who would give us the New Law. Paul writes:

> Why then the law? It was added because of transgressions, till the offspring should come to whom the promise had been made; and it was ordained by angels through an intermediary. Now an intermediary implies more than one; but God is one. Is the law then against the promises of God? Certainly not; for if a law had been given which could make alive, then righteousness would indeed be by the law. But the scripture consigned all things to sin, that what was promised to faith in Jesus Christ might be given to those who believe. Now before faith came, we were confined under the law, kept under restraint until faith should be revealed. So that the law was our custodian until Christ came, that we might be justified by faith. (Gal 3:19–24)

Christ fulfilled the Law, but he did so without nullifying the usefulness of what the Law pointed to and what it taught. A 10 percent tithe is a good model, but it also can be considered a minimum. The Law of Love tells us that giving to others is serving Christ, and giving to the Church is serving his bride. As you seek to evaluate how much you should give to the Church, you may find these Bible verses helpful:

- "Honor the Lord with your wealth, with first

fruits of all your produce; Then will your barns be filled with plenty, with new wine your vats will overflow." (Proverbs 3:9–10, NAB)

- "For where your treasure is, there will your heart be also." (Matthew 6:21)

- "Woe to you, scribes and Pharisees, hypocrites! for you tithe mint and dill and cumin, and have neglected the weightier matters of the law, justice and mercy and faith; these you ought to have done, without neglecting the others." (Matthew 23:23)

- "Consider this: whoever sows sparingly will also reap sparingly, and whoever sows bountifully will also reap bountifully. Each must do as already determined, without sadness or compulsion, for God loves a cheerful giver. Moreover, God is able to make every grace abundant for you, so that in all things, always having all you need, you may have an abundance for every good work." (2 Cor 9:5–8)

But probably nothing is as meaningful to the New Law and tithing than the story of the widow's offering in the Gospel of Mark:

And he sat down opposite the treasury, and watched the multitude putting money into the treasury. Many rich people put in large sums. And a poor widow came, and put in two copper coins, which make a penny. And he called his disciples to him, and said to them, "Truly, I say to you, this poor widow has put in more than all those who are contributing to the treasury. For they all contributed out of their abundance; but she out of her poverty has put in everything she had, her whole living." (Mk 12:41–44)

When it comes to tithing, we really should give all that we reasonably can (and, in different seasons of your life, that may vary). Every Catholic carries the weight of the Church differently and in different amounts. God doesn't demand from us a fixed amount. What he wants is for us to give from the heart, generously, out of love.

That love also expresses itself as a service. Money is not the only way to give: We can also give our time and talent. Consider volunteering for parish events, organizing a small group, or putting in some Sundays with the choir or musicians at Mass if you have the talent (or would like to develop some). Maybe you're an excellent accountant or have studied sacred art. Good news: your parish or a nearby apostolate will accept your help and greatly appreciate your willingness to give what's most precious in life: time.

81

Reject consumerism

Pope John Paul II called it becoming a "slave to possession," and his successor Benedict XVI made similar warnings against rejecting the false idol of materialism. In connection with this, Pope Francis has urged modern Catholics to reject what he calls the "throwaway culture" that finds pleasure in excess spending and acquiring nondurable goods that provide mere temporary happiness. Especially in the modern era, the Church continuously preaches against consumerism.

To be clear, the Church does not stand against the wealthy, and Jesus certainly made no prohibition against prosperity. Recall the story of the rich man, who claims to have observed the entire Law perfectly, asking what else he must do to inherit eternal life. Jesus responds he must sell all he owns, give to the poor, and follow him (Mk 10:17–22). A surface-level, fundamental reading of this passage might cause one to believe that getting into heaven requires all Christians to become completely poor! Of course, that's absurd from a practical and spiritual standpoint. The Holy Family did not reject the great riches given to them at the Nativity, and the coin purse carried by the disciples indicates that the caravan of apostles wasn't completely destitute.

Jesus also had wealthy followers, including Joseph of Arimathea, who provided the tomb for his burial.

Rather than preaching extremism, Christ calls us to balance. In his encounter with the rich young man, Jesus uses this special opportunity, first of all, to point out the rich man's lack of generosity. The rich man believes he has no fault in observing the Law. But the Old Law was one of passivity: Observe these statutes, do no evil, and you can have a clear conscience. The New Law, on the other hand, is the Law of Love, which demands action. Christians are not measured by the evils they resist, but by the loving works they perform. The rich man has much, but the mere thought of sharing what he owns makes him walk away sad.

Therein lies the reason the Church is critical against a culture of consumerism: We can't avoid the good harvest that is a natural reward of hard labor, but our faith teaches that the harvests we reap are not meant solely for our enjoyment. They are for the selfless blessing of others. Consumerism creates discontentedness. We become greedy. Envy drives our spending habits. Tithing and selfless generosity become an afterthought. Bundle up all of this, and consumerism distorts human relationships, creating rivalry with neighbors as we measure others according to what they have rather than who they are. And like the rich man, our wealth becomes an antithesis to generosity.

Avoiding this attitude is critical for all Catholics, new and old. Take time to evaluate your spending habits. Actively seek opportunities to share your wealth with missionaries, your parish, and the poor strangers in your community. If the culture celebrates a throwaway mentality and material idols, be an activist for the durable culture that sustains life and invests in the kingdom of God.

As you seek to battle consumerism and its effects in your life, I encourage you to bear in mind these passages from Scripture:

- "Not that I speak from want, for I have learned to be content in whatever circumstances I am. I know how to get along with humble means, and I also know how to live in prosperity; in any and every circumstance I have learned the secret of being filled and going hungry, both of having abundance and suffering need. I can do all things through Him who strengthens me." (Philippians 4:11–13)

- "And my God will meet all your needs according to the riches of his glory in Christ Jesus." (Philippians 4:19)

Knowing and Defending Your Faith

82

Become an apologist

Understanding the Catholic Faith is simple when we understand the difference between things that are complex and things that are complicated. Look at the difference between a roller coaster and a mechanical watch.

A roller coaster is complex. Building and maintaining a roller coaster requires a team of subject-matter experts: scientists to develop new tech for a more exciting experience; engineers to design the machine; safety specialists to evaluate; logisticians to find supplies; acquisition personnel to buy those supplies; business analysts to determine the cost versus benefit; and a number of other people who provide input in order for decisions to be made. One person cannot understand, beyond appreciation, how the roller coaster is built and maintained.

A watch, on the other hand, is complicated. When one looks at a mechanical watch, it might look intimidating. At first glance, the layers of springs, gears, arms, and other parts look like a jumbled mess. But when she studies them, an observer can learn which spring provides movement to a gear, and how it in turn moves another — eventually understanding the design that's used to turn the second, minute, and hour hands at just the right speeds to be a reliable watch.

The Catholic Faith is complicated, but it is not complex. This means it can be understood. With diligent study, you can know, explain, and defend your Catholic faith. It does not take a master's degree or a PhD, just humility and the willingness to apply yourself to learn. This is important, because in our age of skepticism and general rejection of Christian values, the evangelization to which all Christians are called requires an adequate ability to explain and defend our Catholic faith. To help you, this entire section of this book is dedicated to providing you critical tools for knowing and sharing your faith.

No matter how thoroughly you read this section or other apologetic resources, sooner or later you will still run into a question you don't know the answer to. It's instinctive to us nowadays to go straight to the internet for answers, and that's not a bad place to start. But you probably know someone who has been misinformed by misreporting, fallen for a scam online, or mistaken a satirical website for a credible source. (Maybe that someone is you.) And there are plenty of heretical or counterfeit apologists on the internet.

Ideally, you want to get your information from a trusted source that provides quality, orthodox explanations of the Faith. Look for books and online articles that contain the words "imprimatur" and "nihil obstat." These labels authoritatively assure orthodoxy and freedom from error. And look within the content itself: Is the author or publication presenting its own arguments, or is it explaining and quoting an extant document of the Catholic Magisterium?

Some of the sources I trust the most are Catholic Answers, Eternal Word Television Network (EWTN), Sophia Institute Press, Envoy Institute, Our Sunday Visitor, Ignatius Press, and the *National Catholic Register*. This is an abbreviated list; there are many more excellent places to find quality apologetics. But what's even better is that these are open-door organizations. Almost all of them have a write-in service, a call-in radio show, or a separate place to have a Q&A with an apologist. And you're not just getting Joe the Intern to look up the answer in the *Catechism* — you can actually correspond with and talk to apologists like Patrick Madrid, Tim Staples, Jon Martignoni, Jerry Usher, Father Larry Richards, Jimmy Akin, and many others who are highly trusted in their field.

When you have a question you just cannot find an answer to on a trusted website or in your collection of Catholic books, you can always call or write to these organizations to get your answer. Sometimes they might need to call you back, but they exist to aid you in your walk with Christ by helping you understand the Faith. Call and talk to an apologist who has put decades into their study to find reliable answers to the important questions.

83

Read the Church Fathers

Being able to defend your faith well is crucial to an apostolic and responsible life as a Catholic. While there's no set way to do it, there's a particular area of study that will help you immensely. No, you don't need to go back to school to earn a degree in theology — you just need to read the early Church Fathers.

"The Church Fathers" is the collective name for a number of men who were the intellectual leaders of the first several centuries of the Church. Some were bishops or popes, several were canonized saints, and some were prolific apologists and theologians. Staunch defenders of the Faith, they wrote in extensive detail about what the early Church believed. Because of their apostolic connections, and therefore their inherited orthodoxy, their writings have significant authority and trustworthiness.

Most apologetic arguments with non-Catholic Christians will be based on a disagreement over what this or that verse in the Bible truly means. Are there real effects of baptism? What did Jesus mean when he commanded us to eat his flesh? Are priests able to forgive sins, and is there a biblical basis for it? The testimony of the Church Fathers illustrates how Scripture has been interpreted by the apostles who sat at Christ's feet and their disciples in unbroken succession. They provide firsthand knowledge of what the earliest Christians believed.

Here's one example: Jesus taught his apostle John. Later on, after Jesus ascended into heaven, John taught the Faith to a new disciple named Ignatius. Ignatius became the third bishop of Antioch and composed several epistles on the topics of the sacraments, the duties of a bishop, and the Incarnation. He even used the word "Catholic." If we back up a little, we see that the apostle John also taught the Faith to a man named Polycarp, who became the bishop of Smyrna. Polycarp also wrote many epistles that were read throughout the Church and passed the faith to a young Christian named Irenaeus, who became a bishop in Gaul (in modern-day France). Irenaeus wrote a lengthy apologetic defense that came to be known as *Against Heresies*, and he argued that the Gospels of Matthew, Mark, Luke, and John should be recognized as canonical.

The timeline here is not made up: It is a real, historical line of faithful Christians who passed the Faith from one generation to the next. The first Christians had no doubts about how to determine which was the true Church and which doctrines were the true teachings of Christ. The test was simple: Trace the apostolic succession of the claimants.

So the next time you're entering into that debate with your friend over the proper interpretation of Paul's words to the Corinthians — "The cup of blessing which we bless, is it not a participation in the blood of Christ? The bread which we break, is it not a participation in the body of Christ?" (1 Cor 10:16) — you can tell them that Irenaeus, nearly 150 years later, was making the same argument: "But vain in every respect are they who despise the entire dispensation of God, and disallow the salvation of the flesh, and treat with contempt its regeneration, maintaining that it is not capable of incorruption. But if this indeed does not attain salvation, then neither did the Lord redeem us with his blood, nor is the cup of the Eucharist the communion of his blood, nor the bread which we break the communion of His body."[37]

And if they're still not convinced, tell them about the writings of Ignatius of Antioch, who also wrote a letter to the Romans that describes the Eucharist even more vividly: "I have no delight in corruptible food, nor in the pleasures of this life. I desire the bread of God, the heavenly bread, the bread of life, which is the flesh of Jesus Christ, the Son of God, who became afterwards of the seed of David and Abraham; and I desire the drink of God, namely his blood, which is incorruptible love and eternal life."[38]

Remember, the Church Fathers lived close to the time of Jesus and his apostles. Some were handed the Faith by the apostles themselves. Read their writings to strengthen your own faith, and maybe you can win a little ground in the hearts and minds of your friends as well. At the very least, hopefully you plant seeds. In any case, knowing the Church Fathers makes for highly effective apologetics.

You can find the writings of many Church Fathers online, including such notables as: Clement of Rome (d. 99), Ignatius (d. 110), Polycarp (d. 155), Justin Martyr (the Church's first major lay apologist; d. 165), Irenaeus (d. 202), Cyprian (d. 258), Athanasius (d. 373), Basil (d. 379), Cyril of Jerusalem (d. 386), Ambrose (d. 397), John Chrysostom (d. 407), Jerome (d. 420), Augustine (d. 430), Cyril of Alexandria (d. 444), Pope Leo the Great (d. 461), and Pope Gregory the Great (d. 604).

84

Can we prove that God exists?

The 2015 Pew Religious Landscape survey reported that 22.8 percent of the American population is religiously unaffiliated; atheists made up 3.1 percent and agnostics made up 4 percent of the U.S. population.[39] That means that almost a third of the population in the United States is not active in any faith. Affiliation among Catholics has also declined about 5 percent in the last ten years, according to the same study. Militant atheists tend to be among the loudest voices, particularly in the political sphere, lobbying for anti-Christian laws and removing any sign of God from schools, courts, businesses, and speech.

The prevailing reason there are so many skeptics and non-believers in our time is the belief that science has all the answers. Science is wonderful, and the Church is no enemy of the sciences. Unfortunately, in our time of such technological achievement, many are convinced that empirical science is the only science that can provide answers. Simply put, if it isn't observable, it doesn't exist. Modern atheists toss out logic and philosophy, but they're left with fewer answers because of it. Paradoxically, science needs the philosophy atheists reject. That is, it is a philosophical idea to posit that empirical science is the only way to gain understanding.

You'll need to speak up from time to time, and philosophy and logic are your best tools. You can start with the Five Ways to prove God's existence, as argued by Saint Thomas Aquinas in his famous *Summa Theologiae*. I'll address them briefly here, but it's worth reading more in-depth before you try to argue with an atheist.

The first way we know God exists is by "motion." Where motion exists, there must be something moving it. All things are set in motion by another, but there cannot be, by that very rule, an infinite set of movers; there has to be a prime and first act of motion that is itself unmoved. This is God.

The second is "efficient cause." Like motion, we can observe effects in the universe and easily deduce that each effect has a cause. That cause is itself an effect of another cause; we can't observe any particular thing which caused itself to be. Ultimately, there must be a first cause which is uncaused. This is God.

The third is what philosophy calls "contingency." Many things in the universe that exist are contingent — they are not necessary, but they are possible. Furthermore, contingent things undergo change. Consider a marble slab that is carved into a sculpture. It was always possible for the sculpture to be made from the material, but in order for it to finally exist, the material underwent a change. That change is unnecessary: It never *needed* to happen, but it did. Obviously, contingent things in the universe — like the sculpture — do exist, so there must have been a thing in the universe which was itself necessary and noncontingent to bring these contingent things into existence. Contingent things can create more contingent things, but the existence of even the first contingent thing in a series must ultimately be traced back to something necessary. Therefore, with anything that is unnecessary but still exists, we can deduce that a necessary thing brought it into being. This necessary being is God.

Fourth is "gradation," or the degrees of perfection in which things are observed. In all things, we find varying levels of good and better, more and less, and so on, which are smaller levels of an "utmost" in their category. There are levels of beauty, levels of light, levels of love; but we can only measure things if there is a best, or a perfect, or an utmost, to measure them against. This utmost is God.

Finally, the fifth proof is the observation of "governance" in the world. Things in the world act in specific ways as if they are programmed or governed, like a computer. Every computer has a program which requires intelligence — an intelligent programmer. This is God.

These Five Ways all point to the existence of God from basic, natural principles that everyone can identify and agree upon. They are helpful knowledge for all of us, and even if they do not convince people immediately that God exists, they are a good place to start. Do some research into other arguments, and remember that conversions don't result only from argument. We need to be able to point to proofs that God exists, while remembering that faith is a gift from God. Even as we argue, we should be praying for faith for those who do not believe.

85
What the Church teaches about evolution

Scientific inquiry in the nineteenth and twentieth centuries gave popularity to theories of human evolution. The theory frightens a good number of Christians, who worry that if evolution is true, then the creation account in Scripture must be false. Yet as Catholics, we recognize that creation and evolution can complement each other. The *Catechism* provides the Catholic framework for understanding creation:

> Catechesis on creation is of major importance. It concerns the very foundations of human and Christian life: for it makes explicit the response of the Christian faith to the basic question that men of all times have asked themselves: "Where do we come from?" "Where are we going?" "What is our origin?" "What is our end?" "Where does everything that exists come from and where is it going?" The two questions, the first about the origin and the second about the

273

end, are inseparable. They are decisive for the
meaning and orientation of our life and actions. (282)

The Catholic Church is not opposed to science. From Aristotle
to Galileo and into the modern age, the Church welcomes every legitimate scientific inquiry. At the same time, the Catholic
Church is not in the position to affirm the facts of natural sciences. It is not the Church's mission to judge the natural world
for mankind. In addition, the natural sciences are not firm; scientists are always discovering new things that upend previously held ideas about the way the world works. In the twenty-first
century, scientists continue to make groundbreaking discoveries about matter and time, principles we considered to be reasonably understood not long ago. In short, the Church must
distinguish the thing (evolution) from knowledge of the thing
(what we happen to know at a particular time).

So, what does the Magisterium teach about evolution? Cal-
culatedly little. Evolutionary theories cannot contradict three
truths: (1) Evolution cannot happen without God's sovereignty;
(2) evolution did not produce the human soul; (3) man has a
soul. These principles were mostly developed by Pius XII in his
1950 encyclical *Humani Generis*. The *Catechism* touches on the
subject of these "modern discussions" too (referring to mainstream scientific discoveries and theories): "The question about
the origins of the world and of man has been the object of many
scientific studies which have splendidly enriched our knowledge
of the age and dimensions of the cosmos, the development of
life-forms and the appearance of man. These discoveries invite
us to even greater admiration for the greatness of the Creator,
prompting us to give him thanks for all his works and for the
understanding and wisdom he gives to scholars and researchers"
(283).

What does this mean for us as Catholics? It indicates that we have a certain freedom to believe in evolutionary theories, as long as they advance the understanding of creation and the human person. But we cannot accept those theories that oppose what we know about nature, creation, and the human person. In particular, we cannot accept theories that posit that man was created without God's sovereignty (by accident), or that reject the reality that God has given man an immortal soul. Ultimately, for the Catholic, evolution is a scientific theory that explores how God might have created us; it is really all about him.

86

Defend against *sola scriptura* with confidence

Protestantism is built on the doctrine of *sola scriptura*, which is Latin for "Scripture alone." There are some variations to its application and finality, but in general, this doctrine holds that the Bible alone is the final (or only) authority for Christians, and that within its pages is everything a person needs to know about salvation, truth, and morals.

As far as basics are concerned, all adherents to *sola scriptura* accept at least three core beliefs:

1. The Bible contains all the books that God intended (no more and no less).
2. The Bible is infallible.
3. Each Christian, with the aid of the Holy Spirit, is able to interpret and understand the Scriptures without error.

Perhaps you're wondering what we as Catholics actually believe about the authority of Scripture. The *Catechism* says: "The

Church, to whom the transmission and interpretation of Revelation is entrusted, 'does not derive her certainty about all revealed truths from the holy Scriptures alone. Both Scripture and Tradition must be accepted and honored with equal sentiments of devotion and reverence'" (82). Tradition (with a capital "T") is the transmission of Christ's teaching to the Church through his apostles and their successors (see CCC 75–79).

If you're scratching your head, wondering what Tradition is, don't scratch too hard. Tradition, or Sacred Tradition, is a tricky idea and can leave you scratching for a good while. That's because it cannot be pinned down to a specific thing, time, event, or list. The best way to think of Tradition is to think of its source: Jesus Christ. In him and through him, the entire revelation of God is summed up and fulfilled, foretold by the prophets, preached to the apostles, and commanded to be transmitted to the world. Catholics look to Scripture and Tradition for authority, not Scripture alone.

Your future dialogue and debates about Catholicism with Evangelical Protestants will likely revolve primarily around whether or not a particular teaching is biblical. Depending on the person and their denomination, they will apply this test to every theological belief and religious practice, from purgatory to the Sunday Mass obligation. In order to respond to your Protestant friends' questions, you'll need to be able to push back on the doctrine of *sola scriptura*. Here are a few ways to refute this teaching:

- First, if the Bible is the only basis of instruction for salvation in the Christian faith, then the Bible would need to have been available and readable for all Christians immediately after the Ascension of Christ. Yet the Gospels did not exist for the first several decades after those events took place, and the Church flourished further without a universally agreed-upon canon of Scripture for three and a half centuries. Demonstrating the basis for which books belong in the Bible is impossible without appealing to the external teaching body (or the Church's Magisterium), which determined the list.

- In addition, the belief that the Bible contains everything a person needs to know about salvation, truth, and morals, is not a teaching we find in the Bible. The usual citation is 2 Timothy 3:16, "All Scripture is inspired by God and profitable for teaching, for reproof, for correction, and for training in righteousness"; but this verse does not say that Scripture is the sole source of authority. *Sola scriptura* in itself is an extrabiblical teaching.

- Finally, the belief that each Christian is able to interpret the Scriptures without error would imply that each Christian would arrive at the same truth by reading and analyzing the Bible. Yet the number of Protestant denominations, each of which came about because of a theological disagreement with another church, contradicts this claim.

The best way to defend against *sola scriptura* is to start with the points raised here, but posed as questions. Let your friends examine these and come to the conclusion on their own (but help them get there). After this, a great course of action is to tell them about the early Church Fathers (see section 83). These men defended the Church or discussed Church teachings in harmony with one another before the Bible was assembled. On Scripture, Saint Augustine, who is also a great resource for many Evangelicals, said: "I would not believe in the Gospels were it not for the authority of the Catholic Church."[40]

Is everything we believe as Catholics found in Scripture? Well, yes and no. Everything we believe is found in the Bible, either explicitly or implicitly. For example, we know that baptism is necessary for salvation (Jn 3:1–5; Acts 2:38), and that the Eucharist is the Body and Blood of Christ because the Bible explicitly teaches this (Jn 6:41–56; 1 Cor 1:16, 11:27). We also know that the Bible does not contain words like "the Trinity" and "transubstantiation," but these teachings are implied. Make sure you know where you find your beliefs in the Bible — not only to show your biblical literacy, but to provide common ground with your Protestant friends.

Sacred Tradition and Sacred Scripture, together, flow from the same wellspring, Jesus, but are two distinct modes of transmission. To synthesize select paragraphs from the *Catechism*, the Scriptures are the speech of God as it is put down in writing under the breath of the Holy Spirit. This is different from Tradition, which is the oral transmission of the entire Church — her doctrine, life, and worship — by the apostles and their successors through the Holy Spirit (CCC 79–82).

87

Know your heresies

What is heresy? The *Catechism* states, "*Heresy* is the obstinate postbaptismal denial of some truth which must be believed with divine and catholic faith, or it is likewise an obstinate doubt concerning the same; *apostasy* is the total repudiation of the Christian faith; *schism* is the refusal of submission to the Roman Pontiff or of communion with the members of the Church subject to him" (2089).

Various heresies that plagued the Church in her early centuries subtly resurface from age to age, and it's vital that you grasp what these heresies were (are) so that you will know where the errors are in modern theological debates.

- **Gnosticism**: The Gnostics believed that matter is evil, mostly referring to the material side of the human person. Gnosticism contradicts Genesis 1:31 ("And God saw everything that he had made, and behold, it was very good") and other Scriptures, and denies the Incarnation. If matter is evil, then Jesus Christ could not be true God and true man — for Christ is in no way evil. Thus many Gnostics denied the Incarnation, claiming that Christ only appeared to be a man; his humanity was an illusion.

- **Montanism**: Montanus was an early preacher who was concerned with the gifts of the Holy Spirit. He was doing great, until he preached that anyone who did not receive extraordinary spiritual gifts was not truly a Christian, and further preached that he spoke for the Holy Spirit.

- **Arianism**: Arius, a priest of the fourth century, taught that Jesus was a man created by God in time and with no divine nature. His heresies (and the drawn-out, dramatic debates that resulted) are the primary reason the Church formulated the Nicene Creed, which clarifies the personhood of Christ and the Holy Spirit. (This is the creed we usually pray at Mass.)

- **Pelagianism**: Pelagius denied that man inherits original sin, saying that we become sinful only through the bad example of the corrupt community into which we are born. Moreover, he denied that Christians inherit righteousness as a result of Christ's death on the cross. He said we become personally righteous by instruction and imitation in the Christian community, following the example of Christ. Pelagius stated that man is born morally neutral and can achieve heaven under his own powers. According to him, God's grace is not truly necessary; it merely makes easier an otherwise arduous task.

- **Semi-Pelagianism**: Some people followed a revised form of Pelagius's theology. This effort, too, ended in heresy by claiming that humans can reach out to God under their own power, without God's grace; that once a person has entered a state of grace, one can retain it through one's efforts, without further grace from God.

- **Nestorianism**: This one has to do with both Mary and Jesus. Nestorius denied Mary the title of *Theotokos* (Greek for "God-bearer" or, less literally, "Mother of God"). He claimed that she only bore Christ's human nature in her womb. His theory would fracture Christ into two separate persons (one human and the other divine), only one of whom was in her womb. The Church defined and clarified that referring to Mary as the "Mother of God" is appropriate, not in the sense that she is older than God or the source of God — but rather, meaning that the person she carried in her womb was, in fact, God incarnate. The inverse of this heresy, that Christ had only a single nature, was touted by the Monophysites.

- **Iconoclasm**: Iconoclasts (the word means "image-breaker") claimed that it was sinful to make pictures and statues of Christ and the saints, despite the fact that in the Bible, God had commanded the making of religious icons and statues (see Ex 25:18–20; 1 Chr 28:18–19), including symbolic representations of Christ (cf. Nm 21:8–9 with Jn 3:14).

- **Albigensianism**: The Albigensians taught, in the vein of Gnosticism, that the human soul was created by God and was good, but the body was created by an evil god, and the spirit must be freed from the body. Having children was one of the greatest evils, since it entailed "imprisoning" another "spirit" in flesh. This heresy was also rife with errors regarding morality, such as abandoning marriage.

You may be able to identify these heresies or vestiges of them in modern groups like the Mormons, the Jehovah's Witnesses, and others. You might even see these ideas creep into online forums or elsewhere by well-intentioned but poorly informed Catholics. Heresies have been with the Church since the beginning, but they provide the opportunity to clarify, define, and further understand the Faith. Happily, as the Church preaches the Gospel, we have two golden promises from our Lord. First, he said, "You are Peter, and on this rock I will build my Church, and the gates of Hades shall not prevail against it" (Mt 16:18). He also said that "the Counselor, the Holy Spirit, whom the Father will send in my name, he will teach you all things, and bring to your remembrance all that I have said to you" (Jn 14:26).

88

Veneration vs. worship: An important distinction

You've probably heard at least once (or maybe believed yourself) that Catholics worship the saints and Mary. The short answer is no, we don't; the long answer involves a couple of vocabulary words.

Repeat after me: *Latria* is worship, and *dulia* is veneration. Say it over and over: *latria* and *dulia*; *latria* and *dulia*. Let me explain.

Catholics worship God alone. Period. We worship no other gods, no other holy people, no other objects, nothing. We refer to this worship by the Greek word *latria* — the worship given to God alone.

Catholics love their saints. We don't worship saints — we don't give the saints *latria*, but we venerate (or honor) the saints. The honor we show the saints is *dulia*.

So, why the confusion? We have to rewind the lexicology a little.

The word "worship" has endured some changes in meaning in the English language. The word "worship" comes from *weorth-*

scipe (or worthship) in Old English, which means the condition of being worthy of honor, respect, or dignity. To worship, in the older, larger sense, is to ascribe honor, worth, or excellence to someone, whether a sage, a magistrate, or God. Because of this, and because English is the language closely associated with Protestantism in the West, non-Catholics will often see the honor and respect we give to the saints and have no other word to call it but worship. The word "venerate" really isn't used much outside of Catholicism, so you see the dilemma. Not to mention, most denominations that don't have the Sacrifice of the Mass refer to worship as song, praise, and prayer. So when they hear that we pray with the saints, they naturally assume we are worshiping them. These things cause Protestants and other non-Catholics to believe that Catholics are idolaters.

This allows us to make a distinction. When Catholics participate in the eternal sacrifice at Mass (i.e., when we worship) we adore God. But when we venerate the saints, we honor them.

What do we mean by this "honor"? We mean it in a few different ways. If I want to honor my father, I follow him, I continue his work, and I imitate him. Apply this to the saints: I want to imitate them, I want to believe how they believed, I want to continue their mission, and I want to love Jesus and seek him as they did. That is veneration. Our "devotions" to the saints are about honoring them and seeking to imitate them.

Having said that, we believe that the Church in heaven is the same Church as here on earth; the whole Church is made up not only of us living, the Church Militant (still fighting), but also the Church Suffering (the souls in purgatory, whom we pray for), and the Church Triumphant (those in heaven who see the face of God). Since the souls of the Church Triumphant are with God in heaven, we also believe that we may ask for their prayers, just as we ask those around us in the Church Militant to pray for us.

Be assured that this is deeply rooted in the Bible. Paul writes extensively about spiritual imitation. He states: "I urge you, then, be imitators of me. Therefore, I sent to you Timothy, my beloved and faithful child in the Lord, to remind you of my ways in Christ, as I teach them everywhere in every church" (1 Cor 4:16–17). He says again to the Corinthians: "Be imitators of me, as I am of Christ. I commend you because you remember me in everything and maintain the traditions even as I have delivered them to you" (1 Cor 11:1–2). To the Hebrews, Saint Paul also stresses the importance of imitating true spiritual leaders: "Remember your leaders, those who spoke to you the word of God; consider the outcome of their life and imitate their faith" (Heb 13:7).

Hebrews contains one of the most important passages on imitation: "Therefore, since we are surrounded by so great a cloud of witnesses, let us also lay aside every weight, and sin which clings so closely, and let us run with perseverance the race that is set before us" (12:1) — the race that the saints themselves have already completed.

When someone asks why you worship the saints, understand the difference between *latria* and *dulia*, worship and veneration, and you'll be set. Oh, one more thing: Mary. She's special — "hyper" special. Therefore, we say that unto her, we render *hyperdulia*. Another fancy Greek word, it simply means "more" dulia. We give her more veneration because of her unique place in salvation history. She is truly favored by God among all women, as the angel Gabriel told her (Lk 1:28), so we believe she is. And she foretold that all generations will call her blessed (Lk 1:48), so we do.

89

What is the Immaculate Conception?

Among the priceless paintings, sculptures, and artifacts in the Musei Vaticani (the Vatican Museum, one of the most popular Vatican tours), one can view the Room of the Immaculate Conception. When tourists gather in this room, a common misconception is cleared up: The Immaculate Conception doesn't refer to Jesus, but to Mary, his mother.

Pope Pius IX promulgated the dogma of the Immaculate Conception in 1854, declaring: "We declare, pronounce, and define that the doctrine which holds that the most Blessed Virgin Mary, in the first instance of her conception, by a singular grace and privilege granted by Almighty God, in view of the merits of Jesus Christ, the Savior of the human race, was preserved free from all stain of original sin, is a doctrine revealed by God and therefore to be believed firmly and constantly by all the faithful."[41]

You might be told that the teaching is just a Catholic "invention," but the dogma has significant roots in Sacred Scripture, was attested to by the earliest of Christians, and has been continually stated by the most respected theologians of each age.

Let's start with the biblical evidence. After falling into sin and dragging humanity with them, Adam and Eve were given a promise. God told the serpent, "I will put enmity between you and the woman, and between your seed and her seed; he shall bruise your head, and you shall bruise his heel" (Gn 3:15). This verse refers to Jesus and Mary, the new Adam and the new Eve. The most influential Christian theologians of the second century (and many since then) interpreted Scripture in this way, including Saints Irenaeus, Epiphanius, and Cyprian.

The New Testament also contains a critical reference to Mary's holy uniqueness. In Luke 1:28, the angel Gabriel greets Mary, saying, "Hail, full of grace!" Where the angel says "full of grace," theologians say that Mary's state of grace proceeded from God's pleasure, as all graces do. We believe that this unique perfection of grace bestowed upon her is both intensive and extensive — that is, she was perfect throughout her whole life.[42]

Saint Augustine wrote around 415 that all must confess their sins "except the Holy Virgin Mary, whom I desire, for the sake of the honor of the Lord, to leave entirely out of the question, when the talk is of sin."[43] Saint Ephrem taught around the year 360 that "Mary and Eve, two people without guilt, two simple people, were identical. Later, however, one became the cause of our death, the other the cause of our life."[44]

Defending the Immaculate Conception may come in the form of preemptive questions, too. Your friend might ask you, "If Paul says, 'all have sinned' (Rom 3:23), then how can you say Mary didn't?" This is a great question, but there's a good answer for it: If this verse is to be applied universally, then why wouldn't it apply to Jesus also? Yes, he's God, but he is also considered by theologians of every age to be the "second Adam." So if Jesus is free of sin as the "second Adam," then one can argue the fitness of Mary, the "second Eve," being sinless as well. Moreover, it is fitting to believe in the power of God to preserve a human from sin.

For the sake of consistency, too, remember that Job "was blameless and upright; he feared God and shunned evil" (Job 1:1), and before him was Noah, "a righteous man, blameless in his generation" (Gn 6:9). Both renditions of "blameless" are rendered better as "perfect," and their particular Hebrew words mean "spotless," "undefiled," "without blame," and "complete." If these special figures can be described with these words, then how much more favored was Mary, who was chosen from all women (Lk 1:41) to be the new Ark of the Covenant?

The conversation will continue from there, and you'll be prompted to study up, but this should provide you with a solid and simple basis to defend a highly misunderstood dogma. Do your part to protect this most profound truth of our faith, and let your new appreciation of the uniqueness of Mary bring you ever closer to Jesus.

90

Why can't women be priests?

Why can't women be priests? This topic covers a vast area. It's also a great question! It delves into the nature of man, and why God made men and women. It also touches on discipline, Tradition, and the proper and iconic nature of the priesthood.

Foremost, Christ had a deep love and respect for women. He talked to them in public (Lk 7:11–17), forgave their sins (Jn 8:3–11), served them, allowed them — regardless of their circumstance — to serve him, and called them to become his disciples (Lk 10:39). These are just some examples of his radical treatment of women for his time. Literally, he put his life on the line for them: He is the absolute champion of the respect and dignity owed to women.

Jesus also chose twelve apostles and gave them specific and unambiguous authority, including the authority to "bind and loose" (Mt 16:18; 18:18), to forgive and retain sins (Jn 20:21), and to be equipped for the service of the Church (Eph 4:11). Jesus told them, "He who hears you hears me, and he who rejects you rejects me, and he who rejects me rejects him who sent me" (Lk 10:16). He meant for this authority to be passed on to successors, which we see confirmed in Saint Paul, who states that authority has been granted to him (2 Cor 13:10). But most important, it was the all-male apostles who were present at the Last Supper, which was also the institution of the priesthood. And the Church has preached this position for a very long time. "If anyone shall say that by the words 'Do this in commemoration of me' Christ did not institute the apostles priests, or did not ordain that they and other priests should offer his body and blood: let him be anathema."[45] This power was only given to the apostles, who undeniably were all male.

There's another critical reason why the Church does not ordain women: The Church doesn't have the authority to do so. This teaching was reiterated by Pope Saint John Paul II in his 1994 apostolic letter *Ordinatio Sacerdotalis*, in which he sought to dispel any lingering doubts regarding the Catholic Church's teaching on women's ordination. In it, he writes:

> Although the teaching that priestly ordination is to be reserved to men alone has been preserved by the constant and universal Tradition of the Church and firmly taught by the Magisterium in its more recent documents, at the present time in some places it is nonetheless considered still open to debate, or the Church's judgment that women are not to be admitted to ordination is considered to have a merely disciplinary force.
>
> Wherefore, in order that all doubt may be removed regarding a matter of great importance, a matter which pertains to the Church's divine constitution itself, in virtue of my min-

istry of confirming the brethren (cf. Lk 22:32) I
declare that the Church has no authority whatsoever to confer priestly ordination on women
and that this judgment is to be definitively held
by all the Church's faithful.[46]

Those are very direct words: The Catholic Church has no authority to change what a priest is or who may become a priest,
male or female. But the important thing to remember is that the
priesthood isn't just the special ability (and responsibility) to offer sacrifice; it's also standing in place of Christ (*alter Christi*),
and all who receive Holy Orders are ministering in the person
of Christ (*in persona Christi*). At Mass, we Catholics believe that
it is not just a man in fancy garments offering a sacrifice: We
believe that it is Jesus who presides invisibly over every Eucharistic celebration (CCC 1348). In this vein, since Christ came as
a male, it is proper and fitting that priests and bishops offering
the sacrifice are also male.

The question of why women can't be priests also hints at a
philosophical nuance of our current culture: the belief that the
former lines of sex and gender, which have changed in our social
structure and policy, should also change in our religious insti-
tutions. In short, women should be able to do whatever men do.
Yet this understanding flies in the face of what the priesthood
actually is — and the dignity of women as upheld by the Church.
The priesthood isn't simply a role or a job; it is an ontological
reality, just as maleness and femaleness are realities rooted in
the person. Women cannot be priests any more than men can
be mothers! God has given men and women separate gifts, and
both are critical for our Church and our world.

91
Papal impeccability and other common misconceptions

At some point, you'll need to know how to deflect other common misconceptions about the Catholic Church. Below are some of the ones you'll encounter the most. The good news is, you can respond to each of them with just a little bit of knowledge and rehearsal.

PAPAL IMPECCABILITY

The Church does not, despite the common misconception, believe that papal infallibility means the pope is never wrong—a position which is called papal impeccability. The pope is human, and popes can err, despite their position and despite any personal sanctity. Wearing a white cassock never exempts a person from speaking inaccurately about a Church teaching, quoting incorrectly, or disagreeing with another pope, and it especially never prevents a pope from sinning.

The Catholic Church defines three conditions under which

the pope is infallible: (1) The Pope must be making a decree on matters of faith or morals; (2) the declaration must be binding on the whole Church; and (3) the Pope must be speaking with the full authority of the papacy, and not in a personal capacity.

It is intensely deliberate and specific when the occasion does arise. For example, when the doctrine of the Assumption of Mary was defined by Pope Pius XII in 1950, the Apostolic Constitution *Munificentissimus Deus* took extreme care to explain the complete background, facts, and interpretations of the bodily assumption of Mary into heaven since the beginning of the Church. The document concludes with this statement: "We pronounce, declare, and define it to be a divinely revealed dogma: that the Immaculate Mother of God, the ever Virgin Mary, having completed the course of her earthly life, was assumed body and soul into heavenly glory."

The item in question was a matter of faith, the document states its binding nature explicitly, and the declaration was made by the pope in the full authority of his position.

CONSTANTINE INVENTED THE CATHOLIC CHURCH

Constantine approved and legalized Christianity with the Edict of Milan, which removed penalties for professing Christianity. Later, in 325, he convened the first ecumenical Council of Nicaea to stop Arianism, a heresy that was spreading like a plague in the Church at the time. Because of the importance of this council and the Edict of Milan, many people believe that Constantine "created" the Church.

Yet we know that there were Christians spreading the Gospel since the Ascension and Pentecost around the year 33, and those Christians unanimously believed and wrote about the same things the Church believes today, including the priesthood and the importance of celibacy; the seven sacraments; the pope and the authority of the bishops in communion with him; and holy water — they even crossed themselves. And they called themselves "Catholic."

THE CHURCH DISCOURAGES READING THE BIBLE

The Church, born from the faith of Abraham, Moses, and the prophets, profoundly reveres Scripture as the written word of God. The problem is, who determines what is and what is not the written word of God? That question troubled the Church in the second through the fourth centuries. The FedEx truck didn't drop off copies of the Bible to the apostles at Pentecost — someone had to decide what the Bible was!

In the first few centuries A.D., there was discussion and debate as to what books could be read in Mass and which ones were of the highest authority. Many excellent scholars and Church Fathers proposed their suggested canons with well-reasoned criteria for their selections, but the very first Christian canon was approved for general Christian use by the Catholic Councils of Hippo (393) and Carthage (397). At the time, monks and clergy were the dominant readers of the Bible because they were usually the only ones who were educated enough to read.

The misconception also comes from the accusation that the Church chained up the Bible so Christians could not read it. Manuscripts of Sacred Scripture were sometimes chained up, but that was to keep them from being stolen. These Bibles were copied entirely by hand and were very expensive, making them valuable to looters and thieves. Bibles were often chained to a desk so that everyone could read them.

There's also the fable that the Church placed the Bible on the list of forbidden books. The first "Index" or catalog of forbidden books was published in 1559 by the Sacred Congregation of the Roman Inquisition, a precursor to the Congregation for the Doctrine of the Faith. Any Bibles placed on the index were Protestant versions, usually lacking the deuterocanonical books, or poorly — and thus unreliably — translated.

The Church and the saints emphasize the Bible and exhort the faithful to read the Scriptures daily. Period.

CATHOLICS AREN'T CHRISTIANS

Catholics are the very first Christians. We believe that Jesus Christ is God made man, who came to earth to bring salvation to the whole human race. In early Christian writings, anyone can see clearly that the faith and teachings are the same as the Catholic Church today. Readers will encounter bishops and priests, virgins living in a community (nuns), the Eucharist, confession and absolution, the baptism of infants, the bishop of Rome as head of the Christian religion, and veneration of the saints.

***

These are some of the most common misconceptions you'll encounter, but you'll want to be completely ready to take on any challenge to your faith, so don't stop with this short list. Keep learning!

92

Discover Church history

One of the things that's never failed to increase my faith and appreciation for the Catholic Church is visiting sites that still contain artifacts of the ancient Church. More specifically, I mean seeing the remnants of the ancient Church: ancient mosaics, underground foundations of churches used in antiquity, or the excavated remains of an ancient "house-church."

The experience is eye-opening. Apostolic succession or the communion of saints can begin to seem like vague, irrelevant concepts when we read about them, but that changes when you visit the historical sites of our faith. When you see an ancient house-church in the Holy Land and find where the residents chiseled the sign of the cross into the stone walls, you realize that you share a deep and meaningful connection with them. The same happens when you visit the basement of an ancient church, where you find mosaic floors, frescoed walls, and perhaps even an antique altar. You, many hundreds of years later, are visiting the place where the Faith was just getting started, and yet those Christians believed everything you believe. At this moment you feel like you've been passed a spiritual baton that says, "This is the only thing that will outlast us — this faith, symbolized by these walls and painted plaster." It's humbling in the sweetest of ways, and it changes you.

Your local diocese probably doesn't have a church that dates back to the medieval era or a baroque-style apse to appreciate as a holy work of art. Don't worry — your diocese probably has a crypt, at least, in its cathedral. And other parts of your diocese, or even a museum in the nearest big city, probably do have ancient relics, recovered mosaics or frescoes of Renaissance artists, some liturgical item that was brought over from the Holy Land or Rome, or some room that a saint lived in. These artifacts are everywhere, just waiting for you to come see them.

Get out and see the most ancient Christian objects and places you can. Maybe it means a pilgrimage, or a quick detour on a road trip, or an afternoon excursion on a family vacation. When you see what other Christians saw and where they worshiped, and are able to touch or view their handwritten Bibles and their hand-painted hymn books, or see a monstrance from before the Renaissance, your faith will begin to mature. You'll have a visual reference for ideas like apostolic succession because you stood in the place where generations of bishops shepherded their flocks. You'll have a deeper faith in the communion of saints because you'll realize you're now following in their footsteps. Go see the ancient Church, even if it's just a few generations old, and let your faith grow through the experience.

Evangelization:
It's for Everyone

93

Share the Good News with other Catholics

The Church in our day — our true home and our mother — is hurting. It's a reality of the time we live in, and the Church needs you to do your part to bring about healing and restoration within the Church, and to draw souls to the salvation that can only be found in her. The Church needs men and women who are willing to have the hard conversations about the sins of our leaders. She requires the people who fill the pews to be prepared and willing to defend the Faith. And she absolutely needs you and me to pray, diligently, for the conversion of sinners — Catholic and non-Catholic alike.

Many Christians (both Catholics and non-Catholics) make the mistake of thinking that we should be focused only on gaining converts, convincing people to join our particular church. While this is extremely worthwhile, it is critical to ensure your car works before offering someone else a ride.

What does this mean? It means that your first task as a Catholic is to evangelize other Catholics. You might be thrilled about your faith or have a genuine desire for holiness, but the fact is that many Catholics share neither your enthusiasm nor your ambition. So, you have an opportunity and a call to invite them to go deeper.

I would say, as a convert, that it can be much easier to talk to Catholics than to non-Catholics or atheists about our faith. Yes, in some cases, lapsed Catholics may be bitter about this topic or that; but they, too, have been sealed with the Holy Spirit in baptism — and hopefully the Sacrament of Confirmation, perhaps Holy Matrimony — and they have consumed Jesus Christ, almighty God, present in the Eucharist. You have all the graces on your side. And who better to spend time evangelizing than those members of our family who are lonely, who are hurting, who are in need of encouragement or love and friendship?

To accomplish this task, you must begin to form authentic relationships. Begin by really, genuinely caring about the folks next to you. As trust builds, so does your ability to communicate the joy of the Gospel, and so does their confidence that your spiritual guidance is worthwhile and trustworthy. Forming genuine personal relationships — even with folks who appear to be far from interested in Jesus and the Catholic Church — is the basis of real evangelization. Each Catholic you meet is an opportunity to strengthen the Church, either by combining effort with other energetic and faithful Catholics, or by sharing the fullness of God's love with the lapsed.

94

What is the New Evangelization?

The term "New Evangelization" is one you've likely heard before reading this book. It is an ongoing topic of many Catholic books, Catholic websites, and Catholic blogs, with good reason. But what is it?

The phrase itself is interesting. "New" implies that there was a first and older evangelization, and it suggests that the old way of evangelizing is no longer acceptable, or at least no longer effective. To understand what "new" means in this context, it's helpful to understand what one Catholic author, Eric Sammons, refers to as the "Old Evangelization": the basic principles of evangelization which originated with Jesus himself. The apostles and disciples boldly proclaimed the kerygma (the Gospel message) and the life of Jesus Christ, often through one-on-one relationships.

What, then, is the New Evangelization? We are in a new era of the Church. Much of the evangelized world is experiencing the decline of Christian values and rejection of Christian truths. The assumption that most of our society is Christian or has an essentially Christian worldview is vanishing. People are leaving the Church in masses, and this problem is furthered by grave acts of abuse and scandal in the Church's recent history. Understanding this, Pope Saint John Paul II called for the "New Evangelization," which recognizes the millions of baptized Catholics who have not been brought to encounter with Christ. These neighbors in the pew next to us are the new focus of our evangelistic efforts.

Many ideas have been suggested for achieving an effective New Evangelization. Some seek to imitate the efforts of Protestant megachurches. It is undeniable that these churches have experienced outstanding success in attendance, growing in faith and knowledge, and a heightened active participation among their members. Adopting or Catholicizing these methods and practices is something the Council Fathers of Vatican II clarify in their wisdom: "Nor should we forget that anything wrought by the grace of the Holy Spirit in the hearts of our separated brethren can be a help to our own edification. Whatever is truly Christian is never contrary to what genuinely belongs to the faith; indeed, it can always bring a deeper realization of the mystery of Christ and the Church."[47]

Pope Saint Paul VI, John Paul II's predecessor, also understood the importance of evangelization in the modern era. In his famous apostolic exhortation, *Evangelii Nuntiandi*, he clarifies the most critical principles of evangelization in the modern era of the Church:

> For the Church, evangelizing means bringing the Good News into all the strata of humanity, and through its influence transforming humanity from within and making it new. ... There is no true evangelization if the name, the teaching, the life, the promises, the kingdom and the mystery of Jesus of Nazareth, the Son of God are

not proclaimed. ... Above all the Gospel must
be proclaimed by witness. ... As evangelizers,
we must offer Christ's faithful not the image
of people divided and separated by unedify-
ing quarrels, but the image of people who are
mature in faith and capable of finding a meet-
ing-point beyond the real tensions, thanks to
a shared, sincere and disinterested search for
truth. Yes, the destiny of evangelization is certainly bound up with the witness of unity given
by the Church. ... At this point we wish to emphasize the sign of unity among all Christians
as the way and instrument of evangelization.
The division among Christians is a serious reality which impedes the very work of Christ.[48]

Evangelization cannot occur without preaching, teaching, and
maintaining a wholesome interest in unity. We can do all of
these, but our goal should not be a tidier and more attractive
church, a better experience for Catholics and non-Catholics, or a
more theologically trained laity. The efforts of all evangelism are
centered on a conversion of the heart. John Paul II writes,

Passing from principles, from the obligations of
the Christian conscience, to the actual practice
of the ecumenical journey towards unity, the
Second Vatican Council emphasizes above all
the need for interior conversion. The messian-
ic proclamation that "the time is fulfilled and
the Kingdom of God is at hand," and the sub-
sequent call to "repent, and believe in the Gospel" (Mark 1:15) with which Jesus begins his
mission, indicate the essential element of every

new beginning: the fundamental need for evangelization at every stage of the Church's journey of salvation. This is true in a special way of the process begun by the Second Vatican Council, when it indicated as a dimension of renewal the ecumenical task of uniting divided Christians. "There can be no ecumenism worthy of the name without a change of heart."[49]

Does the teaching of the New Evangelization imply that there are two separate, nonintersecting schools of thought? Is the New Evangelization superior to, or devoid of, the principles of the Old Evangelization? Hardly. There is a New Evangelization, but the methods of yesterday are still vital to its successful end. Far from being the work of priests and dedicated missionaries, now more than ever, the evangelization of Catholics in addition to non-Catholics must be the effort of each one of us.

95

Watch or read a good conversion story

From the writings of Saint Augustine to the modern classics, conversion stories aid us in self-examination, empathy, inspiration, and anticipation. When we read about the conversion of another, first of all we go into self-examination mode. We hear a story that's similar to ours, and we begin to ask ourselves questions. Perhaps these are questions we've already answered or issues we've responded to, but they are presented in a way that uncovers a misunderstanding, confirms a good motive, or identifies a subtle detail that encourages us to think differently and perhaps examine our conscience anew.

Similarly, conversion stories also stir up empathy. Everyone likes a compelling story of change, overcoming obstacles, and dealing with a real-world dilemma. Everyone loves these stories because they remind us of our own lives, triggering empathy — that interior sense of "Hey, I'm not the only one." We are moved to be more attentive, leading to the next item: inspiration. When we're inspired, we act. Conversion stories have no shortage of the inspiration of the Holy Spirit, and he's able to guide us to nearly infinite possibilities.

Another benefit of conversion stories is anticipation. I use this word in two ways. First, by reading or listening to someone tell their story, we're equipped to anticipate better the challenges we're going to face. We get a spiritual and practical "heads up" that makes the difficulties we will meet in our life of faith just a little more bearable. And sometimes, we're given a road map for how to navigate these treacherous roads. Second, these stories often send us into excitement about being or becoming Catholic. Conversion stories can give us the proper appreciation we need to take our faith to the next level.

Whether it's the ancient but still influential *Confessions* by Saint Augustine, the modern story *Crossing the Tiber* by Steve Ray, or any one of the hundreds of hour-long stories you can watch online from *The Journey Home*, I highly recommend you give yourself the benefit of listening to another person explain the motives and challenges of their conversion experience.

96

Evangelize using these simple actions

Evangelization is much easier than most people think, and it's a bit more commonsense than we make it out to be. It doesn't take a deep thinker, an established theologian, or an employed pastor to evangelize — it only takes initiative. Here are a few situations you will probably find yourself in, and how you might use them as an opportunity to evangelize the culture around you.

TELL PEOPLE WHAT YOU ARE DOING

You're about to join, you just have joined, or you are returning to the Catholic Church: the Church that the Son of God founded, through whom all things were made; the oldest surviving institution in the history of humanity; the most controversial and countercultural body of people on the planet. We believe that our God died voluntarily for us. We believe that God entrusted his flock to men in an unbroken and unaltered succession. We believe that we can pray with saints. We believe that God chooses to forgive our sins through the ministry of men who stand in the place of his Son. We believe that water may wash away the original sin that stains our nature. We believe that God commanded us to eat his flesh and drink his blood. We trust in a pretty radical set of beliefs!

Folks these days rarely hear about the Catholic Church from something other than their newsfeed, but you have the opportunity to be a living witness, explaining to them your reasons for believing and the benefits you enjoy. You might want to let them know about the Eucharist, baptism, anointing of the sick, the pope, and so on.

You've embarked on the most excellent adventure and challenge. Be compelled to share this with people. You'll be surprised how many will become quickly engaged by your enthusiasm, and you might even be able to bring a few of them home. Maybe thousands — it's up to you.

SPEAK UP WHEN SOMEONE MISREPRESENTS THE CHURCH

"The pope said this the other day." "The Catholic Church believes in that." "Catholics don't do such and such." Many statements your friends, family, or coworkers make about Catholicism might be completely wrong, so who's going to correct them if not you? It takes a bit of work, as well as active participation in the Catholic media and basic apologetics, but when someone misquotes the pope or misrepresents the Catholic Church's teachings, you can say something. It won't help to be confrontational about it; just be gentle and generously informative.

TELL PEOPLE YOU'RE PRAYING FOR THEM

I've met a lot of anti-Catholics or people who refuse to go to Church anymore — even atheists who will denounce any form of religion — but I have yet to run into someone who disfavored a prayer. Prayer can serve as an encouragement to those who are unwilling to do it themselves. The thing is, you actually have to pray. Just saying you're going to pray or that you are "praying" when someone is under stress, hardship, or despair is as good as telling your children you're feeding them while they sit at a plateless table. While you're praying for others, especially those who do not pray for themselves, pray that they will receive the grace to pray as well.

GIVE AWAY YOUR RESOURCES

Remember that book you read — the one that really helped you in that time of need, or spiritual dryness, or addiction? You can't keep it to yourself. Buy a second copy if you absolutely have to have it, but if you're not going to reread it, give it to someone else instead of letting it collect dust. Even if you're going to reread it, lend it out to someone. Sometimes giving people an "I need that back by" date will take it from last to first on their reading list. And remember that great article you saw online? Share it. You'll be surprised how far that reaches folks when you don't know what they're struggling with.

HELP SOMEONE

Call them "random acts of kindness" if you want, but don't make them random: Perform regular acts of kindness. Someone trying to reach the top shelf but can't? Help them. A friend struggling with bills? Give them some money. Older lady having trouble with groceries? Stop watching and help her. Last parking spot left? Let someone else have that front row spot at the grocery store. When these moments come along, some people will notice your actions and say, "Why'd you do that?" That's your chance to tell them about the joy that's inside of you (1 Pt 3:16). You don't have to be a preacher; just tell them you believe that serving others is the best way to serve God.

QUOTE THE BIBLE

It's not too popular among Catholics because we don't use the Bible as a source of proof texting our faith. But we should all be able to quote the Bible in times of joy, adversity, or confusion. A solid and appropriate Bible verse is the unshakable and timely voice of God, and God's word was meant to be shared. Its wisdom is unquestionably enduring, its encouragement is remarkably beneficial, and its moral guidance is everlasting. When possible, quote God's word; his words are immeasurably more useful than any others.

JUST SPEND TIME WITH PEOPLE

Rather than chatting on the Xbox or passing funny emails at work, actually spend quality time with your friends, coworkers, and people you meet. Praying for them in private is great, but being there for them, sharing your life with them, and listening to them is worlds more effective than hoping they'll "come around." And who knows, maybe you'll be the one who gets evangelized because you never knew they were Catholic, too!

CHOOSE YOUR ATTITUDE

Few things are easier to choose than an attitude. The ability to evangelize well is highly dependent on this choice. People generally like listening to people who don't come off as critical, arrogant, defensive, irritated, presumptuous, or ungrateful. One of your greatest weapons in the culture war is the attitude you have. Other than being careful to avoid the attitudes I just mentioned, it's important to also choose the way you respond. It needs to be positive, balanced, unemotional, and overall authentic. When you get the opportunity to evangelize, your best tactic is preaching out of love. Saint Francis de Sales presents profound words to help us understand this: "Whoever preaches with love, preaches sufficiently against heresy, although he may not utter a word of controversy. This is not my opinion only, but that of the most celebrated preachers I know."[50]

There's no silver bullet to evangelize, no magic wand to wave over people to get them to go to Church with you. It just takes caring and noticing opportunities. Ask God to highlight these for you, and I guarantee he will not fail you. The only catch: When he shows you what he wants, you need to be ready to act on his inspiration.

97
Become a philosopher

As Christians, we have Christ's Great Commission, which is our directive to make disciples of all nations through preaching the word of God and through baptism. The word "evangelism" is derived from the Greek "*eu*," meaning good, and "*angelia*," meaning message. Hence, the evangelist is one who literally spreads the good message, which we call the Gospel.

What makes a good evangelist? A smart and effective evangelist is a bright and capable apologist. In the Greek, *apologia* means to give a reasoned defense, usually a legal argument, complete with evidence that would support one's position. Because Christianity is a conversion-centric religion, evangelists have to be armed with the arguments to invite, or rather compel, someone to convert.

What makes a good, well-reasoned defense of the Faith? It's important to have an understanding of Sacred Scripture, as well as knowledge of the Church Fathers. But another, often overlooked, ingredient is a good grasp of philosophy. Many would-be apologists study the arguments already presented by generations of apologists, but issues evolve and change over time. New worldviews, new ideologies, new challenges, and even new religions appear. It takes new arguments and strategies to compellingly invite others to join the Christian ranks, and making these arguments requires some philosophy.

Philosophy, which literally means "love of wisdom," differs from theology in its approach to fundamental questions. Philosophy assumes no direct revelation from God, while theology presupposes not only God's existence, but also that knowledge given to us through revelation. One might look for a theological answer to "Does God exist?" and find that people's revelatory experiences are valid, proving God's existence — or that the Bible, as the inspired word of God, tells us that God exists. Philosophy, on the other hand, approaches the question without such assumptions. A philosopher seeks to answer the question of God's existence utilizing human reason.

There are four key areas in which the study of philosophy can aid a Catholic in evangelizing the culture:

1. **To combat atheism**. Atheism does not merely say God does not exist, but instead maintains that one can know there is not a God. (Whereas an agnostic may still choose to believe or not, an atheist has made a firm commitment.) Because the atheist is only debating the existence of God rather than the finer points of theology, philosophy helps us meet the atheist on his own ground. We can learn how to provide logical arguments that build on what the atheist believes about the world.

2. **To help answer the problem of evil.** No topic threatens the inner life of faith more than that of evil and suffering. Individual sins and temptations come and go, but suffering lingers like a dull ache — or, worse, a scar that doesn't heal. Understanding

what suffering truly is, what pain really means, and how we experience our existence can help us maintain our faith through the most challenging times. The problem of evil and suffering is one of the oldest arguments against hope and faith, and sound philosophy provides some satisfying answers.

3. **To unravel absurdities in heresy.** How does *sola scriptura* play out if taken to its logical conclusion? The Bible doesn't mention this, so how can we think it through logically with what the Bible does say? Without the logic of philosophy, heresies can be combatted only as a faith claim. For this reason, philosophy can help us think through difficult topics and find inconsistencies and absurdities.

4. **To clarify and help our personal faith.** While many Protestants criticize the Catholic Faith for being too mystical and relying too much on the idea of mystery and the unexplainable, the Eastern Orthodox often accuse the Catholic Faith of being too systematic, rational, and not leaving enough mystery. Could it be that Catholicism has struck a balance between the mystical and the rational? *Fides et Ratio*, Pope John Paul II's encyclical on faith and reason, not only helps us understand the intricacies of our personal faith and the Faith we celebrate together, but also gives us a deeper appreciation for our liturgy and grace.

98

Seek reform, not revolution

Martin Luther is credited with launching the Protestant Reformation. In reality, his "reformation" was a revolution in the Church, which led to mass confusion and upheaval that still impacts us today. Luther began with rightly pointing out Church corruption, but he ended up founding a whole new church with a new theology. From there, "reformers" of all sorts started their own congregations: Huldrych Zwingli of Switzerland, Thomas Cranmer of England, Martin Bucer of Germany, and John Knox of Scotland, among dozens of others. Some of these congregations lasted; some didn't.

Many of these would-be reformers, like Luther, turned from honorable means of uprooting corruption to a complete destruction of the faith they had previously professed. No Mass. No Eucharist. No priests. No belief in the real effects of baptism. No Mary. The list goes on. It's true — the Church desperately needed reform at the time — but Protestantism rejected the possibility of reform in favor of all-out revolution.

As Protestant denominations splintered off, what did the Catholic Church herself do to address the issues of corruption, poor education, lack of discipline, absence of virtue, and liturgical variations within her ranks? Well, the Church is a body, and that body urgently and decisively motioned for reform — true reform that would create not division, but unity and personal holiness. The numerous contributors to this movement, known as the Counter-Reformation or the Catholic Reformation, came in all shapes, sizes, and nationalities, with their own gifts and goals to help the Church reform correctly. Robert Bellarmine, Philip Neri, Pius V, and Jane Frances de Chantal are just a few of the key players. It's vital to know not only their names and what they did, but more importantly, what they did not do: revolt.

In their desperate search for trustworthy leadership and holiness, early Protestant "reformers" missed the reality that true reform begins with reforming oneself. As Saint Ignatius of Loyola, one of the first and most influential of the Counter-Reformers, said: "He who goes about to reform the world must begin with himself, or he loses his labor."[51]

Before you and I are ready to tell others how to live the Catholic life, we really need to take a look in the mirror. And before we dust off our pitchforks, demanding change from others, we should look at what change we are in need of. This is exactly the spiritual (and sometimes physical) hypocrisy that Jesus warned us of: "Why do you see the speck that is in your brother's eye, but do not notice the log that is in your own eye? Or how can you say to your brother, 'Let me take the speck out of your eye,' when there is the log in your own eye? You hypocrite, first take the log out of your own eye, and then you will see clearly to take the speck out of your brother's eye" (Mt 7:3–5).

As you proceed in your spiritual journey — and especially as you try to evangelize others in the Church and bring about beneficial change — take a good, honest look at the way you're in need of your own reform. And remember when you do seek change in the Church, whether at a parish level or higher, seek reform, not revolution.

99

Let your silence speak

Perhaps you have heard the popular saying about evangelization, "Preach the Gospel at all times and, when necessary, use words." It has been attributed to Saint Teresa of Calcutta and Saint Francis of Assisi, though there is no proof that either of them ever uttered or wrote the phrase. Some argue that the quote, real or not, results in treating the activity of preaching as a last resort, making for lazy evangelism. Arguments of meaning and source aside, it is a powerful quote that points to a vital part of evangelizing. It correctly identifies the need for us to be excellent examples as Christians before we ever say a word to convince others.

This is an idea we see threaded through the evangelizing counsel of the New Testament:

- "Let your light so shine before men, that they may see your good works and give glory to your Father who is in heaven." (Matthew 5:16)
- "Let no one despise your youth, but set the believers an example in speech and conduct, in love, in faith, in purity." (1 Timothy 4:12)

- "Do your best to present yourself to God as one approved, a workman who has no need to be ashamed, rightly handling the word of truth." (2 Timothy 2:15)

Our actions are essential to our faith, and setting an example as adopted children of God is not just a socially acceptable means of evangelizing. The demonstration of our faith through our life and actions will ultimately determine our merit and salvation. We are reminded by Saint Paul that "we must all appear before the judgment seat of Christ, so that each one may receive good or evil, according to what he has done in the body" (2 Cor 5:10).

At the same time, preaching with words is also important. The importance of effective preaching is evident in the lives of Christ and the saints. They didn't stop with good morals and manners: They frequently challenged the authorities — Jesus overturned the money tables! To take just one example, Saint Francis of Assisi's biographer, Thomas of Celano, wrote that Francis's verbal preaching was convicting, compelling, and almost constant, as he would preach vocally anyplace he could find an audience and a place to stand. But Francis knew, as all the other saints have known, that the life of the preacher must conform the words of the preacher. Saint Francis once said, "All the brothers, however, should preach by their deeds."[52] And there are times when this is actually the best means of evangelizing. To be converted, a soul needs both preaching and evangelization.

This is especially true with our family members and loved ones. Often they don't need more words from us, but they do need our example. After I got into the umpteenth debate with my wife (and many friends) but never really went anywhere, my wife asked me to evangelize with silence. I did. Things began to fall into place. At a dinner with friends who had been instrumental in my conversion, we started to discuss the doctrines on the Blessed Virgin Mary. Something unusual happened that night. My friend made a pithy point on the doctrine of Mary's Immaculate Conception, and my wife, after moments of silence, said, "Wow, I've never heard it explained like that before," in a tone that we all knew implied she had just moved a step closer to Catholicism and trust in the Magisterium.

Often when it comes to the Faith, it can be hardest to believe our loved ones. Really! As much as we love our spouse and friends, often our loved ones need a different voice, a different preacher. A new point of view and a new voice can articulate truth in a fresh new way that doesn't add any pressure.

Silence really can be the best means of evangelism. While we pray for the conversion of our loved ones, we must pray that we become good examples of the faith we want them to accept. At the same time, we can pray for God to place the right person in their life, to whom they can listen with a fresh frame of mind and perhaps be moved closer to the truth.

100

Evangelize your kids

If you have kids, your primary occupation is full-time evangelist. There's no way around it.

Parenthood is fun, but it is also challenging. It can be hard to see the spiritual benefit that parenthood provides to the world, but it's there. When we parents encounter priests and singles who have the mental bandwidth to preach to hundreds or even thousands, it can seem like our efforts to change the world from our own home are futile. But our contribution to the world is more than a few encouraging words of wisdom and truth: It's a generation of Catholic children who, in turn, will be able to preach to others and hand on the Faith to future generations.

By evangelizing our children, we are taking to the front lines of the culture war in a vitally essential way. Here's how Vatican II put it: "Christian husbands and wives are cooperators in grace and witnesses of faith for each other, their children, and all others in their household. They are the first to communicate the faith to their children and to educate them by word and example for the Christian and apostolic life. They prudently help them in the choice of their vocation and carefully promote any sacred vocation which they may discern in them."[53]

If you're wondering where to start when evangelizing your children, I recommend beginning with the documents of Vatican II. Here is a can't-miss quotation that summarizes how to approach your evangelizing efforts:

> Since parents have given children their life, they are bound by the most serious obligation to educate their offspring and therefore must be recognized as the primary and principal educators. This role in education is so important that only with difficulty can it be supplied where it is lacking. Parents are the ones who must create a family atmosphere animated by love and respect for God and man, in which the well-rounded personal and social education of children is fostered. Hence the family is the first school of the social virtues that every society needs. It is particularly in the Christian family, enriched by the grace and office of the sacrament of matrimony, that children should be taught from their early years to have a knowledge of God according to the faith received in baptism, to worship Him, and to love their neighbor. Here, too, they find their first experience of a wholesome human society and of the Church. Finally, it is through the family that they are gradually led to a companionship with their fellowmen and with the people of God. Let parents, then, recognize the inestimable importance a truly Christian family has for the life and progress of God's own people.[54]

We evangelize our children, not just for the good of their own souls, but so they will be equipped to evangelize, too. The documents of Vatican II state, "Children also have their own apostolic work to do. According to their ability they are true living witnesses of Christ among their companions."[55] The thing is, they can't do this without you. Parents are the first and final evangelists. So live your faith wholeheartedly and share the gifts you have received with your children. If you're raising Catholic children, you're doing more work than a single evangelist can in ten lifetimes, because you actually make new lives.

Conclusion
Where to Go from Here

We have covered a lot of ground in this book. I hope you're not too overwhelmed.

What I want you to think right now is not, "Wow, I'd better get started!," or, "Oh no, there's so much to do." Instead, this departing message is essentially the same as the first in this book: Slow down. Christianity is a lifestyle, and as Catholicism is "the fullness of the faith," it takes a lifetime. There's no hurry to get to exotic pilgrimage locations, or to learn Latin. There's still a lot you may want to do, but slowly add these things to your daily routine. Dog-ear this book, pull it out again and again, and be open to discovering something new about your faith each time. You can create a list of goals to cross off one by one, or plan to incorporate one new practice at a time to aid in your spiritual growth. Don't try to do it all at once — it's not possible, and it's not the point.

Finally, keep in mind that there's only one thing you absolutely must do in the Christian life: Constantly continue to be a convert by participating in the sacraments, loving others, and turning your heart toward Jesus. Everything else in this book (I hope!) aids in this, and I earnestly pray it will deepen your life with Christ.

Appendix
Helpful Resources

CHURCH DOCUMENTS

The Enchiridion of Indulgences (as a guide to receiving Indulgences).

Documents of Vatican II. Provides a great deal of understanding the Church in the modern age.

Catechism of the Catholic Church. The best resource for understanding the Catholic Faith.

Compendium to the Catechism of the Catholic Church. A shorter version of the *Catechism.*

THE CATHOLIC LIFE

Catholic Traditions and Treasures, by Helen Hoffner.

Around the Year with the Von Trapp Family, by Maria Von Trapp. Studiously assembled family traditions for the entire liturgical year.

What Catholics Are Free to Believe or Not, by Father H. G. Hughes. Exactly what it sounds like.

The Catholic Church Saved My Marriage, by Dr. David Anders. Discover the hidden grace in the Sacrament of Matrimony.

Life Lessons, by Patrick Madrid. Acclaimed apologist discusses fifty moments that shaped his faith — a good way to learn from the mistakes of others.

Why God Hides, by Father John Portavella. God is not silent — learn how to hear his still, small voice.

Catholic Matters, by Father Richard John Neuhaus. Successfully navigate your way through confusion, controversy, and truth in the Catholic life.

PRAYER, SPIRITUALITY, AND SACRAMENTALS

Summa of the Christian Life, by Venerable Louis of Granada.

Interior Castle, by Saint Teresa of Ávila.

The Contemplative Rosary, by Dan Burke and Connie Rossini. A beautiful, practical guide to deeper reflection with the Rosary.

Holy Water and Its Significance for Catholics, by Rev. Henry Theiler. Everything you want to know about holy water is in this little book.

The Sign of the Cross, by Bert Ghezzi. Recover the power of ancient prayer in this powerhouse modern classic.

The Spiritual Direction of St. Claude de la Colombiere. An easily digestible read from one of the most famous spiritual directors of all time.

Conversion, by Father Donald Haggerty. A powerful thrust into self-examination and encounter with God.

Introduction to the Devout Life, by Saint Francis de Sales. Consult the spiritual life with the saint that guided numerous souls.

The Imitation of Christ, by Thomas à Kempis. Numerous saints remarked that this is the book that inspired them above all others.

APOLOGETICS AND EXPLAINING THE CATHOLIC FAITH

The Drama of Salvation, by Jimmy Akin. A deep dive into the study of salvation, and what it entails for Catholics.

The Faith of Our Fathers, by James Cardinal Gibbons. A proven classic that covers numerous topics in ordinary language.

The Fathers of the Church, by Mike Aquilina. The historian discusses and provides testimony of the early Church Fathers, demonstrating that our faith today was the accepted faith of the earliest Christians.

Crossing the Tiber, by Steve Ray. A moving testimony jam-packed with Steve peeling back the onion on Catholic theology.

Surprised by Truth (volumes 1–3), by Patrick Madrid. Three best selling and effective apologetics books that tell the conversion stories of a range of skeptics and how they came to know the truth.

The Protestant's Dilemma, by Devin Rose. Capitalizing on the use of *reductio ad absurdum* (reduction to absurdity), Protestant notions and beliefs are carried out to their logical — and inevitably problematic — consequences.

The "20 Answers" series, by Catholic Answers. From the Eucharist to evolution, you'll get all your answers in these pithy books.

Catholicism and Fundamentalism, by Karl Keating. The author unravels the anti-Catholic arguments of Fundamentalists with their own words.

Behold Your Mother, by Tim Staples. Simply the most thorough and helpful refutation of arguments against the Blessed Virgin Mary available.

Where Is That in the Bible?, Why Is That in Tradition?, and *Answer Me This!,* by Patrick Madrid. Three of the most to-the-point apologetics books, covering a myriad of topics.

The Catholic Controversy, by Saint Francis de Sales. This is the gifted apologist of the Counter-Reformation's single-volume answer to many Protestant notions.

Upon This Rock, by Steve Ray. Using the testimony of the earliest Christian documents to prove the foundations of historic Christian beliefs, Ray also uses Protestant scholars and historians to expose their misuse of history and misunderstanding of Scripture.

Why Catholic Bibles Are Bigger, by Gary Michuta. Most arguments start with Scripture, but most Christians do not understand the history of the Bible. Dismantling common errors about the origins of the Bible, the author shows why the Catholic Bible is the authoritative version for all Christians.

The Fathers Know Best, by Jimmy Akin. A comprehensive assembly of quotes on the early Church Fathers and other early Christian writings, grouped by topic for straightforward reference.

Theology and Sanity, by Frank Sheed. An outstanding means of practically showing how dangerous secular notions are, how much God loves us, and how much we need the Catholic intellect at all times.

Fundamentals of Catholic Dogma, by Ludwig Ott. The secret weapon of every Catholic apologist. Ott offers a historical and academically organized approach to every single article of the Catholic Faith and Tradition.

Sources of Catholic Dogma, by Henry Denzinger. The cover sells itself: "A comprehensive sourcebook on authentic Catholic dogma that is magisterially anchored while at the same time both practical and non-voluminous."

On the Trinity (or *The Trinity*), by Saint Augustine. Considered the authority on the examination and explanation of the Trinity.

Summa Theologiae, by Saint Thomas Aquinas. The master source of virtually every question and answer about Catholic Faith, Tradition, morals, and life. This — though extremely thorough — is a summary of the complete teachings in Thomas's *Summa Contra Gentiles*.

Controversies of the Christian Faith, by Saint Robert Bellarmine.

The architect of modern apologetics and the chief theologian of the Counter-Reformation wrote this three-volume set, which is considered the bedrock on which most apologetic arguments for the Catholic Faith have been formed.

BOOKS ON CHRISTIAN TOPICS

The Handbook of Christian Apologetics, by Peter Kreeft. Sound logic and practical means of dismantling arguments from the existence of God to the authority of the Bible.

Orthodoxy and *The Everlasting Man*, by G. K. Chesterton. Chesterton makes convincing first-person arguments that Christianity is the answer to life's (and humanity's) biggest riddles.

The Case for Christ, by Lee Strobel. An investigative look into the validity of the biblical accounts of Jesus and his existence. Good arguments are also presented for his divinity.

Mere Christianity, by C. S. Lewis. Undeniably one of the most enduring apologetics books of all time, Lewis sows the seeds of doubt in modern skepticism and provides several unique analogies to help understand the Christian faith.

There are so many more books and so many excellent authors, I cannot cover them all. If you can find titles from these authors, you'll be in good hands: Hilaire Belloc, Hans Urs Von Balthasar, Trent Horn, Scott Hahn, Reginald Garrigou LaGrange, Ralph McInerny, Cardinal Joseph Ratzinger (Pope Benedict XVI), Stacy Trasancos, Steve Weidenkopf, Ronald Knox, Mark Brumley, and Edward Feser.

WRITINGS AND LIVES OF THE SAINTS

Excellent resources to learn more about the saints include Butler's *Lives of the Saints* and *The Book of Saints* by Basil Watkins. You might also enjoy the following books.

The autobiography of Saint Margaret Mary Alacoque.

The Life of St. Dominic, by Augusta Drane.

St. Aloysius Gonzaga, by Fr. Maurice Meschler.

John of the Cross: Man and Mystic, by Richard Hardy.

Joan of Arc, by Mark Twain.

St. Francis de Sales, by Louis Stacpoole Kenny.

Confessions, by Saint Augustine.

The Life of St. Philip Neri, by Antonio Gallonio.

Story of a Soul, the autobiography of Saint Thérèse of Lisieux.

The Spiritual Genius of Saint Thérèse of Lisieux, by Jean Guitton.

Hounds of the Lord, by Kevin Vost.

The Curé D'Ars, by Francois Trochu.

Notes

1. Ray Ryland, "Why Is It a Mortal Sin to Miss Mass?", *Catholic Answers* magazine, July, 2000.
2. Code of Canon Law, 919.1.
3. William Saunders, "The Sacred Heart of Jesus," *Arlington Catholic Herald*, October 13, 1994.
4. Pius IX, *Ineffabilis Deus,* December 8, 1854.
5. Second Vatican Council, *Lumen Gentium*, November 21, 1964, 49.
6. Thomas Aquinas, *Summa Theologiae*, Suppl. 72.
7. Tertullian, *De Corona*, chapter 3.
8. Cyril of Jerusalem, "Catechesis," Lecture 13, par. 36.
9. James Gibbons, *The Faith of Our Fathers* (1876; repr., London: Aeterna Press, 2015).
10. Cyril of Jerusalem, "Catechesis," Lecture 13, par. 36.
11. Second Vatican Council, *Lumen Gentium*, 39.
12. Aquinas, *Summa Theologiae*, III:87:3.
13. Teresa of Avila, *Autobiography*, chapter 31.
14. Paul VI, *Indulgentiarum Doctrina*, January 1, 1967, "Norms," n. 1.
15. Ignatius of Antioch, "Epistle to the Ephesians," chapters IV–VI.
16. Paul VI, *Christus Dominus*, October 28, 1965, 2.

17. Pius XII, *Fidei Donum*, April 21, 1957, 42.
18. See Jimmy Akin's "Does God Pick the Pope?" *Catholic Answers*, March 13, 2018, https://www.catholic.com/magazine/online-edition/does-god-pick-the-pope.
19. John Beal, James Coriden, and Thomas Green, eds., *New Commentary on the Code of Canon Law* (Mahwah, NJ: Paulist Press, 2000), 1417.
20. United States Conference of Catholic Bishops, General Instruction of the Roman Missal, 2011, no. 274.
21. Ibid.
22. Ceremonial of Bishops, no. 72.
23. Office for the Liturgical Celebrations of the Supreme Pontiff, "Liturgical Vestments and the Vesting Prayers," Vatican.va.
24. Joseph Ratzinger, Mass homily, April 18, 2005.
25. Fulton Sheen, "Foreword," in Leslie Rumble and Charles Carty, *Radio Replies: First Volume* (St. Paul, MN: TAN Books, 1940).
26. Pew Research Center, "Where the Public Stands on Religious Liberty vs. Nondiscrimination," September 28, 2016, http://www.pewforum.org/.
27. Read the complete story told by my wife and me in *Surprised by Life* (Nashua, NH: Sophia Press, 2017) and *Inseparable* (El Cajon, CA: Catholic Answers Press, 2018).
28. Paul VI, *Humanae Vitae*, July 25, 1968, 10.
29. Didache 2:1–2.
30. Tertullian, *Apology*, 9:8.
31. The National Right to Life Committee, "The State of Abortion in the United States," January 2018, https://www.nrlc.org/uploads/communications/stateofabortion2018.pdf.
32. Centers for Disease Control, "Abortion Surveillance—United States, 2014 Surveillance Summaries," November 24, 2017, 66(24);1–48, MMWR.
33. Congregation for the Doctrine of the Faith, Declaration on Euthanasia, 3.

34. John XXIII, *Pacem in Terris*, April 11, 1963, 25.
35. Ibid., 105–106.
36. Joshua D. Pitts, Kaustav Misra, and Thomas Henry, "The Wages of Religion," International Journal of Business and Social Science 2, no. 14 (2011).
37. Irenaeus, *Against Heresies*, book V, chapter 2.
38. Ignatius of Antioch, "Epistle to the Romans," chapter 7.
39. Pew Research Center, "America's Changing Religious Landscape," May 12, 2015, http://www.pewforum.org.
40. Augustine, Against the Letter of Mani Called "The Foundation," 5:6.
41. Pius IX, *Ineffabilis Deus*.
42. Ludwig Ott, *Fundamentals of Catholic Dogma*, (St. Paul:MN, TAN Books, 2009), 199–201.
43. Augustine, *On Nature and Grace*, chapters 36, 42.
44. Ephrem, Op. Syr., II:37, quoted in Ott, *Fundamentals of Catholic Dogma*, 200.
45. Council of Trent, session 22, chapter 1.
46. John Paul II, *Ordinatio Sacerdotalis*, May 22, 1994, 4.
47. Second Vatican Council, *Unitatis Redintegratio*, November 21, 1964, 4.
48. Paul VI, *Evangelii Nuntiandi*, December 8, 1975, 18, 21, 22, 77.
49. John Paul II, *Ut Unum Sint*, May 25, 1995, 15.
50. Louise Stacpoole-Kenny, *St. Francis de Sales: A Biography of the Gentle Saint* (St. Paul:MN, TAN Books, 2009), 240.
51. Kevin O'Brien, *The Ignatian Adventure: Experiencing the Spiritual Exercises of St. Ignatius* (Chicago: Loyola Press, 2011), 101.
52. Francis of Assisi, *The Earlier Rule*, chapter XVII, par. 1.
53. Second Vatican Council, *Apostolicam Actuositatem*, November 18, 1965, 11.
54. Second Vatican Council, *Gravissimum Educationis*, October 28, 1965, 3.
55. Second Vatican Council, *Apostolicam Actuositatem*, 9.

About the Author

Shaun McAfee is a convert to the Catholic Faith and deeply desires the continual conversion of Catholics to Christ and a deepening of practical faith in the Church. He is the author of *Reform Yourself!* (Catholic Answers Press), *Social Media Magisterium* (En Route), and *Filling Our Father's House* (Sophia Press), among other titles. He is the founder and editor of EpicPew.com, blogs at the *National Catholic Register*, writes for the *Catholic Herald* and *Catholic Answers* magazine, and has written for numerous Catholic resources. He currently lives in Vicenza, Italy, with his wife, Jessica, and four kids, Gabriel, Tristan, Dominic, and Alette.